D0941051

SMITHSONIAN CONTRIBUTIONS TO ANTHROPOLOGY

VOLUME 9

Navajo Political Process

Aubrey W. Williams, Jr.

SMITHSONIAN INSTITUTION PRESS
City of Washington
1970

227197

A Publication of the

SMITHSONIAN INSTITUTION

United States National Museum

LIBRARY OF CONGRESS CATALOG 69-60007

U.S. Government Printing Office, Washington: 1970

For sale by the Superintendent of Documents, U.S. Government Printing Office
Washington, D.C. 20402 - Price $3.75

Meetings

For long time
there have been meetings
of many men
for many days.
At the meetings
there is talking
talking,
talking.
Some this way,
some that way.
In the morning
when my father
leaves for meeting
he says to us,
"When I come here again
then I will know
if it be best
to have many sheep
or a few sheep,
to use the land
or let it sleep."
But
when my father
comes home from meeting
he does not know
which talking way to follow.

Tonight
when my father
came home from meeting
he just sat looking
and looking.
Then my mother
spoke to me.
She said
"A meeting is like rain.
When there is little talk
now and then,
here and there,
it is good.
It makes thoughts grow as
little rain makes corn grow.
But big talk, too much,
is like a flood
taking things of long
standing before it."
My mother
said this to me,
but I think
she wanted my father
to hear it.

Author: Anonymous Navajo

Preface

The purpose of this work is to describe the function of various political structures and their incorporation into the Navajo way of life. The data presented in this study were collected over a 2-year period—January 1961 to December 1963—during which I spent 18 months on the Navajo Reservation and adjoining areas as a participant-observer of Navajo culture. The report was written, in part, while I was in the field in order to utilize both historical and contemporary documents maintained by the Navajo Tribe and the Bureau of Indian Affairs at Window Rock, Arizona.

My introduction to contemporary Navajo life was as an employee of the Navajo Tribe in the capacity of an ethnographer. On January 1, 1961, I became a member of a research team seeking ethnohistorical facts from elderly Navajos to support a land claims case against the U.S. Government. On the afternoon of the day I arrived on the Navajo Reservation, I was "presented" with two 4-wheel-drive Jeeps, two tape recorders, two interpreters, four Navajo helpers, and a list of Navajo place names and personal names which I was to go out and locate and interview on the following day. I was told that I could spend the remainder of the afternoon securing food and provisions for my research team for a 3-week stay in the field. During the next 2 months nearly 150 informants over the age of 60 years were interviewed (a maximum of 14 on any single day) concerning the cultural patterns of their families and relatives as far back in time as each informant was able to remember.

My work with the Navajo Tribe put me in contact with many tribal officials, traders, Bureau of Indian Affairs personnel, missionaries, grazing committee members, and chapter officers in all parts of the Navajo Reservation. The most frequent contact was with chapter officials; we frequently utilized chapter houses as temporary headquarters in our search for informants. In most cases it was necessary to obtain the approval of each chapter's officers before we were allowed to use chapter buildings for interviews and living quarters. I soon learned that obtaining this approval was no mere formality even though we had the general blessings of the Navajo Tribal Council and the approval of the tribal government to conduct such inquiries. Chapter officers almost invariably wanted to know a great deal about what we hoped to do with the information we were planning to collect, and why certain members of their chapter had been named as prospective informants. The independent spirit and actions of each chapter organization aroused my interest and resulted in the study presented here.

I am indebted to a great many people for the information presented herein. Chronologically, I am grateful to David M. Brugge, J. Lee Correll, Clyde Peshlakai, Bernadine Whitegoat, and Maxwell Yazzi who first introduced and interpreted Navajo culture to me on the Navajo Reservation. I am indebted to John Y. Begaye and Ralph Johns who, as tribal employees, allowed me to pester both them and their staffs with questions about Navajo life for over 14 months. I owe a great debt to the hundreds of Navajo men and women who tried to answer my questions concerning the operation of their chapter organization. Thanks are due to Jane Erickson who helped in final proofreading and to Mary Anne Libby who assisted in indexing the study.

My greatest debt is that which I owe to Edward H. Spicer who acted as the supervisor of my graduate studies in the Department of Anthropology at the University of Arizona. I feel certain that without his gentle but persistent demand for the highest possible quality of workmanship both in the field and in writing, the study would not contain what clarity it now possesses.

The research for this paper was financially supported by a Comin's Fund Fellowship from the Department of Anthropology, University of Arizona, for the months of June, July, and August 1961, and the Wenner-Gren Foundation for Anthropological Research fellowship awarded in June 1962. I am also indebted to the Bureau of Ethnic Research, Department of Anthropology, University of Arizona, for the appointment as a Research Assistant on their Navajo Project under the auspices of the National Cancer Institute in the months of October 1962 to May 1963.

Finally, I wish to thank my wife, Rebecca, whose thoughtful evaluation and insight throughout the original formulation, during the many months of field work, and in the countless hours of first, second, and third rewriting phases of the work has been a constant inspiration throughout the total study.

A.W.W.

University of Maryland
College Park, Maryland
31 July 1967

Contents

Illustrations

MAPS

FIGURES

PLATES

(All plates follow page 72)

321-627—70——2

Navajo Political Process

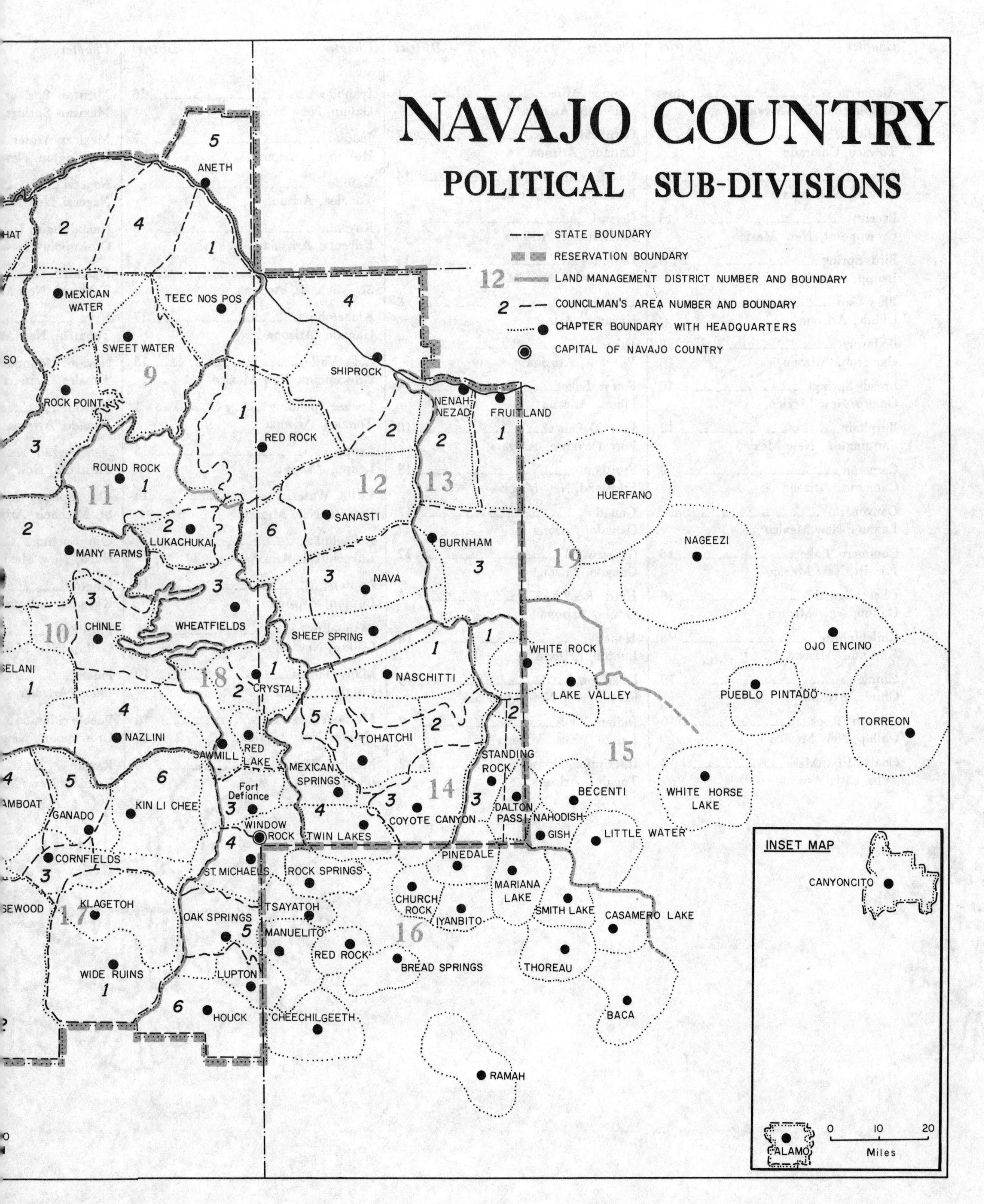

321-627 O - 70 (Face p. 1)

Chapter	*District*
Alamo Magdalena, New Mexico	inset
Aneth Towaco, Colorado	12
Baca Prewitt, New Mexico	16
Becenti Crownpoint, New Mexico	15
Bird Spring Leupp, Arizona	5
Blue Gap Chinle, Arizona	4
Bodaway Cameron, Arizona	3
Bread Springs Gallup, New Mexico	16
Burnham Farmington, New Mexico	13
Cameron Cameron, Arizona	3
Canyoncito Laguna, New Mexico	inset
Casamero Lake Prewitt, New Mexico	16
Cheechilgeeth Gallup, New Mexico	16
Chilchinbito Kayenta, Arizona	8
Chinle Chinle, Arizona	10
Church Rock Gallup, New Mexico	16
Coal Mine Mesa Tuba City, Arizona	3

Chapter	*District*
Copper Mine Cameron, Arizona	1
Cornfields Ganado, Arizona	17
Coyote Canyon Brimhall, New Mexico	14
Crystal Ft. Defiance, Arizona	18
Dalton Pass Crownpoint, New Mexico	15
Dennehotso Kayenta, Arizona	8
Dilcon Winslow, Arizona	7
Forest Lake Piñon, Arizona	4
Fort Defiance Fort Defiance, Arizona	18
Fruitland Fruitland, New Mexico	13
Ganado Ganado, Arizona	17
Greasewood Ganado, Arizona	17
Hard Rock Oraibi, Arizona	4
Houck Lupton, Arizona	18
Huerfano Farmington, New Mexico	19
Indian Wells Indian Wells, Arizona	7
Inscription House Tonalea, Arizona	2

Chapter	*District*
Iyanbito Gallup, New Mexico	16
Jeddito Holbrook, Arizona	7
Kaibito Tonalea, Arizona	1
Kayenta Kayenta, Arizona	8
Kin Li Chee St. Michaels, Arizona	17
Klagetoh Ganado, Arizona	17
Lake Valley Crownpoint, New Mexico	15
Lechee (pending) Tonalea, Arizona	1
Leupp Leupp, Arizona	5
Little Water Prewitt, New Mexico	15
Lukachukai Lukachukai, Arizona	11
Lupton Lupton, Arizona	18
Manuelito Gallup, New Mexico	16
Many Farms Chinle, Arizona	10
Mariana Lake Gallup, New Mexico	16
Mexican Hat Bluff, Utah	8

Chapter
Mexican Springs Mexican Springs,
Mexican Water Farmington, New
Nageezi Nageezi, New Me
Nahodishgish (pe Crownpoint, New
Naschitti Tohatchi, New M
Nava Tohatchi, New M
Navajo Mountain Tonalea, Arizona
Nazlini Ganado, Arizona
Nenahnezad Fruitland, New M
Oak Springs St. Michaels, Ari
Ojo Encino Cuba, New Mexi
Oljeto Kayenta, Arizona
Pinedale Gallup, New Mex
Piñon Piñon, Arizona
Pueblo Pintado Crownpoint, New
Ramah Ramah, New Me

Chapter	District
New Mexico	14
Mexico	9
ico	19
ding) / Mexico	15
exico	14
exico	12
	2
	10
exico	13
ona	18
o	19
	8
co	16
	4
Mexico	15
xico	16

Chapter	District
Red Lake Tonalea, Arizona	1
Red Lake Ft. Defiance, Arizona	18
Red Rock Shiprock, New Mexico	12
Red Rock Ft. Wingate, New Mexico	16
Rock Point Chinle, Arizona	9
Rock Springs Gallup, New Mexico	16
Round Rock Chinle, Arizona	11
Sanasti Shiprock, New Mexico	12
St. Michaels St. Michaels, Arizona	18
Sawmill Sawmill, Arizona	18
Sheep Spring Tohatchi, New Mexico	12
Shiprock Shiprock, New Mexico	12
Shonto Tonalea, Arizona	2
Smith Lake Thoreau, New Mexico	16
Standing Rock Crownpoint, New Mexico	15
Steamboat Ganado, Arizona	17

Chapter	District
Sweet Water Farmington, New Mexico	9
Teec Nos Pos Shiprock, New Mexico	9
Teastoh Winslow, Arizona	7
Thoreau Thoreau, New Mexico	16
Tohatchi Tohatchi, New Mexico	14
Tolani Lake Leupp, Arizona	5
Torreon Cuba, New Mexico	15
Tsayatoh Mentmore, New Mexico	16
Tselani Ganado, Arizona	10
Tuba City Tuba City, Arizona	3
Twin Lakes Gallup, New Mexico	14
Wheatfields Lukachukai, Arizona	11
White Cone Indian Wells, Arizona	7
White Horse Lake Crownpoint, New Mexico	15
White Rock Crownpoint, New Mexico	15
Wide Ruins Chambers, Arizona	17

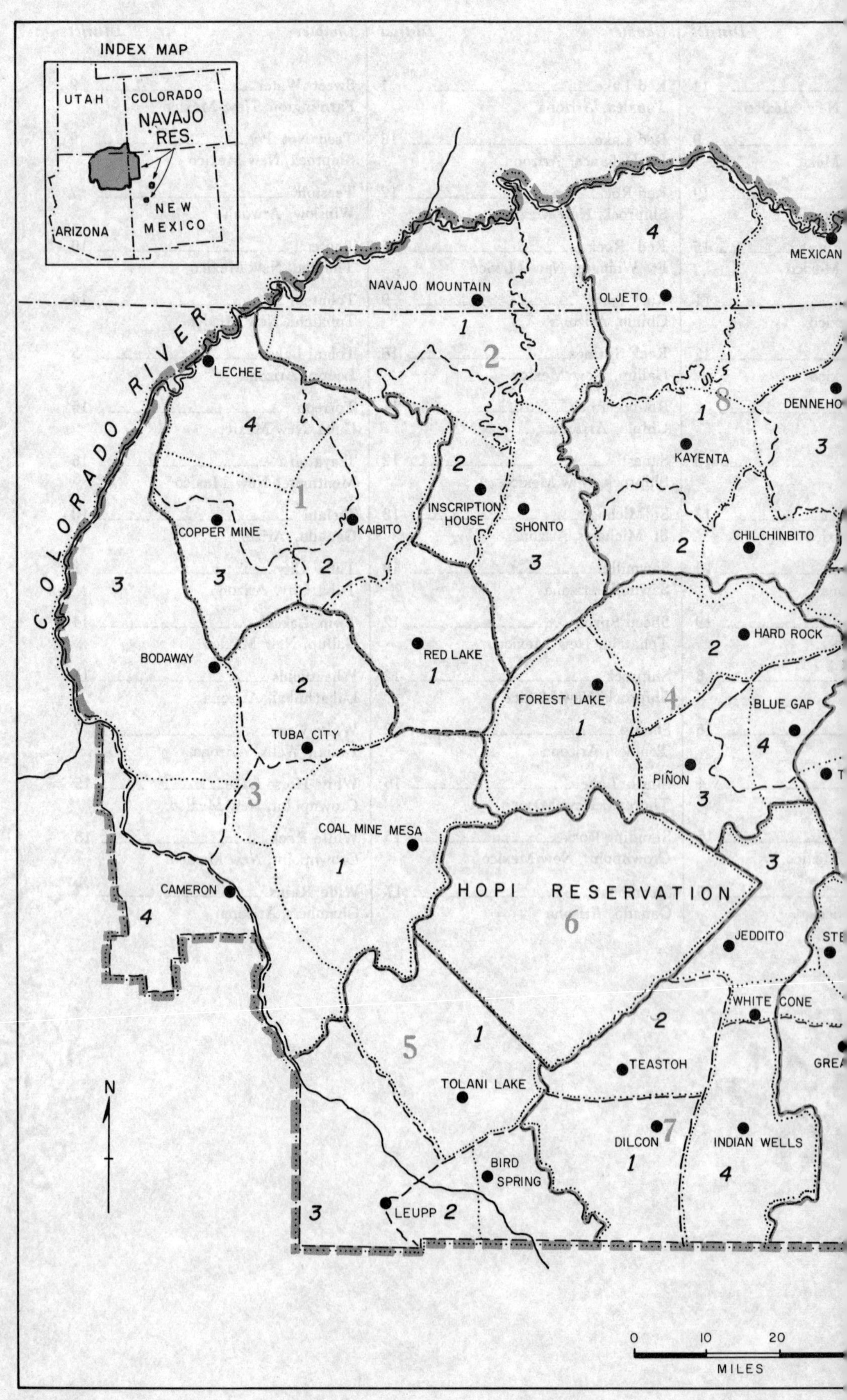

INDEX MAP
UTAH
COLORADO
NAVAJO RES.
ARIZONA
NEW MEXICO
COLORADO RIVER
NAVAJO MOUNTAIN
OLJETO
MEXICAN
LECHEE
KAYENTA
DENNEHO
INSCRIPTION HOUSE
SHONTO
KAIBITO
COPPER MINE
CHILCHINBITO
HARD ROCK
RED LAKE
BODAWAY
FOREST LAKE
BLUE GAP
TUBA CITY
PIÑON
COAL MINE MESA
HOPI RESERVATION
CAMERON
JEDDITO
WHITE CONE
TEASTOH
TOLANI LAKE
DILCON
INDIAN WELLS
BIRD SPRING
LEUPP
N
0 10 20
MILES

Map 1

Perspective

The contemporary culture of the Navajo Indians[1] living in the southwestern part of the United States includes a local political structure that bears striking resemblance to the New England town meeting of the 17th and 18th centuries (Savelle, 1942, pp. 140–143). Among the 95,000 Navajos of today, the local political meeting is known as a "chapter" and there are 96 chapters in Navajo country[2] (map 1). Chapters or community meetings on a more or less scheduled basis were introduced in 1927 by John G. Hunter who was, at the time, the Superintendent of the Leupp Agency (see pl. 1). In recalling his efforts to establish community meetings among the Leupp Navajo, Hunter said:

> I became aware that we [Bureau of Indian Affairs personnel] were not reaching Navajos, except when they came into the Agency's office, or as we went out to them as isolated individuals in the field, and I thought that if I could organize them into community meetings, we could tell them of our [U.S. Government's] programs and we could find out what they wanted. [Interview, 1961.]

Under Hunter's supervision the first chapter was organized on July 20, 1927, and all adult Navajos within the jurisdiction of the Leupp Agency were asked to attend. Hunter recalls that "over 150 Navajo adult men and women attended the first meeting held at the Leupp Agency compound located at Leupp, Arizona" and the "model for this community meeting was the New England town meeting with a set of elected officials" (ibid.). In addition to a successful launching of the first meeting, as measured by the number of Navajos who attended, subsequent meetings had larger numbers of Navajos in attendance. The larger numbers of Navajos at meetings soon proved to be unwieldly, according to Hunter, and "we decided to have meetings in various locations away from Leupp and have one general meeting a year at Leupp" (ibid.). Thus, in 1928, local community meetings with elected officers were organized and established within the Leupp Agency under the guiding hand of Hunter and his assistants. The smaller local community meetings were modeled after the larger and primary meeting held at Leupp, and all elected officers were Navajo men who were chosen to be president, vice-president, or secretary of the respective chapters.

Hunter left the Leupp Agency during 1928 to assume the position of Superintendent of the Southern Navajo Agency at Fort Defiance, Arizona. He estimates that there were 400 to 600 adult Navajos participating in chapter meetings at that time in the Leupp Agency (ibid.). The success attained in organizing and establishing local meetings among the scattered population of Navajos in the Leupp Agency prompted Hunter to organize the Southern Navajo Agency people along the lines developed at Leupp. Hunter states that "as soon as I got my feet on the ground, I began organizing chapters at my new post" (ibid.). The idea of chapters spread to other areas of the Navajo population and by 1934 there were over 500 chapters established.

A number of historical, cultural, geographical, and demographical factors stood in opposition to the estab-

[1] In this study, the Spanish spelling "Navajo" is used in preference to the Anglicized spelling, "Navaho," except where reference is made to titles of organizations, publications, etc., which specifically use the Anglicized spelling. Many authorities (including Kluckhohn, Spencer, Reichard, and the Bureau of American Ethnology) have sought to standardize the Anglicized spelling, while others (such as Underhill, Young, and the officials of the Window Rock administrative offices) appear to prefer the Spanish spelling. The earliest authoritative source on this subject advocated usage of the Anglicized spelling as more easily pronounced, while acknowledging the Spanish spelling as "the older and more correct form" (Franciscan Fathers, 1910, p. 26).

[2] "Navajo country" will be used throughout the text to refer to the Navajo Reservation and those areas adjacent to it on which Navajos live at present (map 2, p. 3).

lishment of local, community-wide, self-governing units for Navajos in 1927. This study neither attempts to restate the history and prehistory of the Navajo people, nor gives an exhaustive treatment of their geography, demography, or culture. An attempt is made to point out the significant factors in these areas, and to establish a sociocultural baseline or cultural position of the Navajo people prior to the development of chapters.

The Navajo Reservation encompasses portions of three States: Arizona, New Mexico, and Utah. The total reservation is nearly 25,000 square miles in size, and is the largest Indian reservation in the United States. At present the Navajo Indians are the most numerous of all the American Indian people, approximately 25 percent of the total Indian population. Robert Young (1961, p. 328) estimates that the Navajo population in 1960 was 93,357.

Geographically, the greater part of the Navajo Reservation is a desert which is frequently bare and barren. It is bisected by a range of mountains that run from northwest to southeast. The northwestern end of this range of mountains is known as Lukachukai, the middle portion is called the Tunicha Range, and the southeastern end is known as the Chuska Range. The upper portions of this range of mountains are covered with growths of ponderosa pine, piñon, and juniper trees which gradually blend in with scrub oak trees at higher elevations and sagebrush at the lower elevations.

The area of Navajo country exceeds more than 16 million acres, and has an average elevation of 6,000 ft. Precipitation falls on Navajo country in two seasons, winter and summer, averaging about 10 inches annually for the whole area. The climate is generally sunny and arid; humid areas within Navajo country are limited to the regions above 7,500 ft. in elevation and comprise only 10 percent of the total land area. These humid sections are not used by Navajos for permanent homesites, but occasionally a family makes their winter camp in these upper elevations in order to be near supplies of wood which are used as fuel for heating hogans or houses and for cooking.

The majority of Navajos live in the broad alluvial valleys and on the upland mesas. These areas generally receive about 12 inches of rain a year, and comprise about 40 percent of the total land area. The rest of the land is an upland desert with only about 8 inches of precipitation annually. Relatively few Navajos live in the desert regions, for water is scarce for humans, domesticated animals upon which many Navajos depend, and plant growth.

The subsistence pattern of most Navajos today includes sheep and goat pastoralism in combination with dry-farm tillage. The principal crop grown is maize. The settlement pattern is primarily that of the isolated hogan [3] camp, which is commonly the dwelling place for an extended family. The camp (two or three hogans) or hogan clusters are hidden from view. The isolated camp of Navajos is a traditional settlement pattern, and its retention is perhaps the most distinctive feature of Navajo culture today.

The cultural history of the Navajo is replete with references concerning the various cultural items and techniques borrowed and incorporated from other people (Vogt, 1961; Underhill, 1956; Hill, 1940a; Van Valkenburg, 1938; and Kluckhohn and Leighton, 1946). Yet each of the historical and cultural accounts cited above mentions the distinctive character of Navajo culture through time, in spite of the influx of ideas from different cultures. It is worth noting that Navajos have not adopted town life as a way of living even though there have been many people around them who live in compact, settled villages. Navajos have selected certain ideas and techniques from other cultures and incorporated them into their own culture, yet disregarded (ignored) other patterns of various contact cultural systems. The fact that the Navajo people were politically independent until 1864—when the U.S. Army defeated them—allowing Navajos to accept or reject differing cultural items on an indirect and permissive basis over a 400-year period, is fundamental (Vogt, 1961, p. 325).

The first description of Navajo culture appears in the 1630 report of Fray Alonzo de Benavides (1945). His report describes the Navajos as skilled farmers who store their grain in a certain kind of hut (Forrestal, 1954, pp. 45–46). Included in the Benavides account in an account of a meeting with several Navajo leaders who had been persuaded to come in and negotiate peace with the Spanish. The Navajo leaders of 1630 spoke of their people as "going about these fields and mountains like deer and jack-rabbits" (Forrestal, 1954, pp. 47–48). This graphic description of Navajo mobility is repeated in accounts some 120 years later, when Navajos were asked to settle down in villages under the guidance of Franciscan missionaries (see p. 4). It is possible that the Navajo leaders were asked in 1630 to bring their people "in" and settle down in villages. The Benavides report also tells of the willingness of Navajos to participate in a trading fair (presumably at a pueblo) to which, in order to show their peaceful intent, they would bring their women and children (Forrestal, 1954, p. 51).

A second picture of Navajo culture is provided by the description in the Rabal documents which cover the period of 1706 to 1743 (Hill 1940a, p. 395). In these documents the Navajo are described as living in small

[3] The hogan or house in which Navajos live is generally a one-room, undivided, circular, log structure with a cribbed log roof which is traditionally covered with about a 1-foot layer of earth.

compact settlements or "rancherias," keeping domesticated horses, sheep, and goats, and raising maize, wheat, and melons. Various students of Navajo culture disagree over the meaning of term "rancherias" as applied to Navajo life. Kluckhohn and Leighton (1946, p. 5) state that it means Navajos were living in compact settlements, but Vogt (1961, p. 294) says "it is very doubtful if Navajos ever lived in compact communities." Keur (1941) finds that although clustering hogans did occur, there was a scattering of them over rocky promontories for distances of one-eighth to one-fourth of a mile, and that these clusterings did not persist much beyond 1812.

Navajo life as described in the Rabal documents is that of a people peacefully pursuing a settled life. Peace between the Spanish and Navajo characterizes the years from 1720 to 1770, and in this period occurred the most successful Spanish attempt to settle Navajos in villages (Reeve, 1960, p. 209).

Contact between the Navajo and Spanish increased during the middle of the 18th century (Vogt, 1961, p. 295) as the former were being pushed out of the *Dinetah,* the location in which they first settled in the Southwest (see map 2). *Dinetah* (in northeastern New Mexico) is bounded on the east by the Chama River, on the north by the San Juan River, and on the west by Largo Canyon. To the north of *Dinetah,* and across the San Juan River, lived the Ute Indians who were increasing their raids across the San Juan River into Navajo *Dinetah* (Thomas, 1940, p. 117). Drought also plagued the Navajos in *Dinetah* at this time, according to the report a Taos Indian brought back from his visit to them. The Taos traveler said that the Navajo had lost most of their planted crops and were forced to draw heavily on their cattle and sheep for subsistence (Reeve, 1960, pp. 202, 204). Arid conditions and Ute raids probably contributed to the desire of Navajos to move south toward the slopes of Mount Taylor in north central New Mexico, where a small group of Navajos had moved prior to the large-scale emigration from *Dinetah* (Reeve, 1959, pp. 11, 17, 23).

The southward movement of Navajos brought them in contact with Spanish settlers who were moving west-

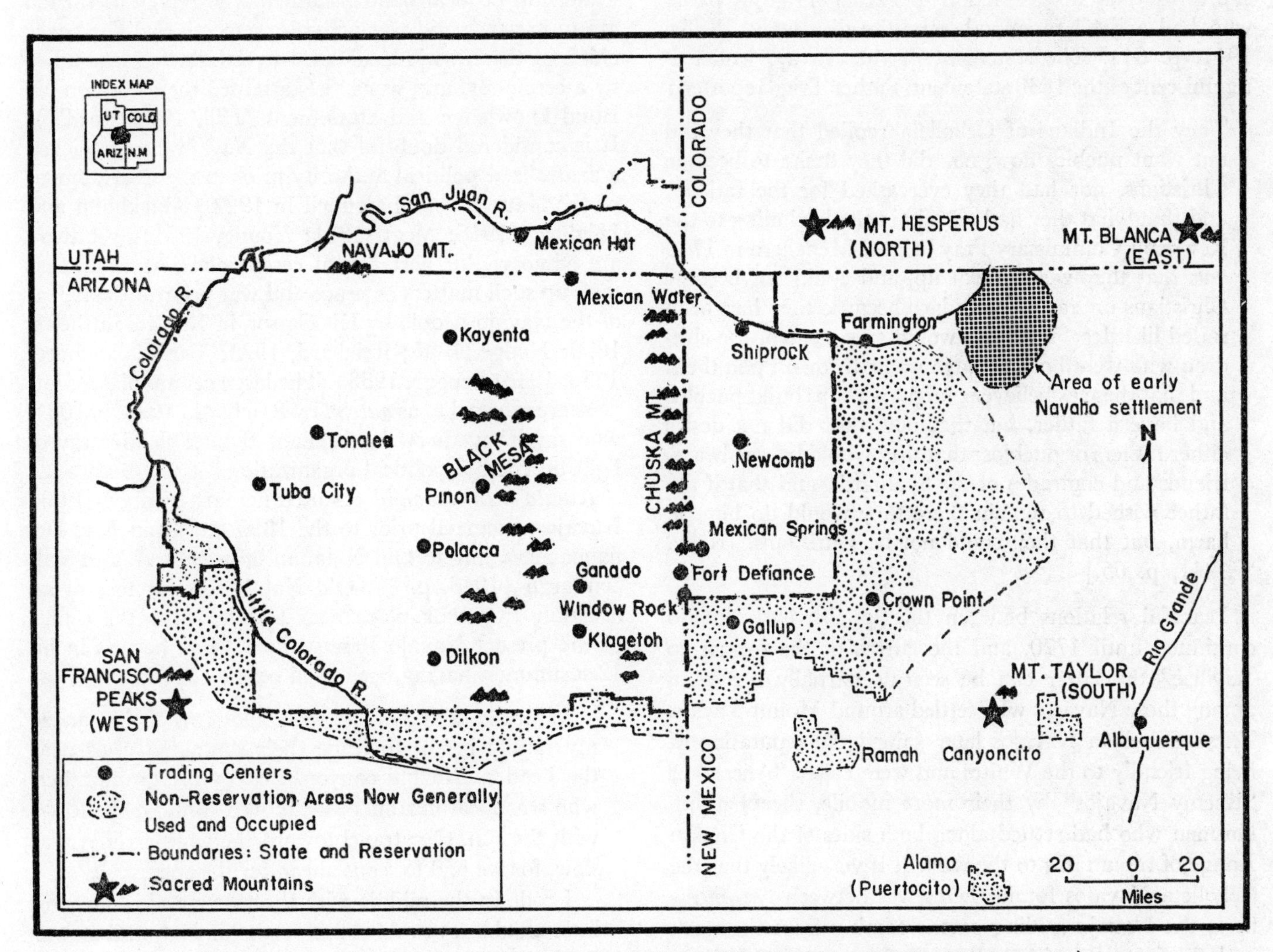

MAP 2.—Navajo country. (U.S.G.S., State, and Navajo Tribe Land Investigation Division maps.)

ward from the Rio Grande. Navajo and Spanish settlers met in the Cebolleta area, which includes Mount Taylor, during the 1740's and 1750's prompting the Spanish Governor, Tomás Veles Cachupin (1749–54), to offer the Navajos an "asylum in permanent settlements in the Rio Abajo." The fugitives, however, were not yet prepared to surrender their mobile way of life in the mountains and mesas of Navajo country (Thomas, 1940, p. 117).

The Spanish were successful, however, in settling a number of Navajos in compact communities in the Cebolleta region during the years 1744 to 1750 (Kelly, 1941, p. 56). It is possible that some of the "refugees" from the north were willing to give up their life in the mountains and mesas and live in villages under the guidance of Fray Juan Miguel Menchero. The Navajos living in groups around one of several missions were to have their children baptized, in return for which the missionaries promised them horses, mules, cows, sheep, clothing, picks, and shovels. A series of difficulties, however, plagued the missionaries' efforts to obtain enough supplies and many promises were broken. In 1750, the Navajos at Cebolleta expressed their dissatisfaction to Father Trigo, a padre who had arrived to smooth over the discontent (Kelly, 1941, p. 64). The statement of the Navajo leader is reminiscent of the 1630 statement. Father Trigo reported:

> They the Indians of Cebolleta replied that they did not want pueblos now, nor did they desire to become Christians, nor had they ever asked for the fathers; and that what they had all said in the beginning to the Reverend Commissary Fray Miguel Menchero in 1746 was that they were grown up, and could not become Christians or stay in one place because they had been raised like deer, that they would give some of the children who were born to have water thrown upon them and that these as believers, might perhaps build pueblos and have a father, but that now they did not desire either fathers or pueblos; that they would be, as always, friends and comrades of the Spaniards, and that if the father wished to remain there they would do him no harm, but that they could not be Christians. [Kelly, 1941, p. 65.]

Peaceful relations between the Spanish and Navajo continued until 1770, and the efforts of the former to "civilize" the latter can be seen as partially successful among those Navajos who settled around Mount Taylor. These Cebolleta Navajos later gained the reputation of being friendly to the Whites and were called "Aliens" or "Enemy Navajos" by their more mobile, sheepherding kinsmen who had settled along both sides of the Chuska Range of mountains to the west. It is very likely that the Cebolleta Navajos found themselves between two crossfires; the Navajo raiding parties coming from the west, and the irate Spanish settlers to the east of Cebolleta. Thus, the "Alien" Navajos remained—for the most part—passive toward both groups.

The Spanish government, as well as the Mexican government which succeeded it in 1821 in New Mexico, employed both punitive raids and diplomacy to stop the Navajos from raiding Spanish settlements. The Spanish and Mexican authorities sought in vain for an overall political leader of the Navajo people with whom they could negotiate peace. At various times, a Navajo leader was selected by the Spanish as the "Paramount Chief of the Navajo Tribe" and showered with gifts and symbols of authority, but rarely did the selected leader command the respect of more than 300 to 400 people (Reeve, 1960). Thus, raids continued to characterize the relations between the Spanish-Mexican people and the Navajo up to, and into, the period of American occupation of the New Mexico Territory in 1846.

The culture of the Navajo at the time of the American entry into the Territory included a settlement pattern of scattered small hogan clusters occupied by matrilocal extended families organized politically under the dual leadership of local band headmen who represented each group in peace and war activities respectively. The peace chiefs of the Navajo local band were inducted into office by a ceremony, and war chiefs attained their position via ritual knowledge and attainment (Hill, 1940b, p. 24). It is considered doubtful that the Navajo ever achieved a centralized political authority prior to the development of the Navajo Tribal Council in 1922 (Kluckhohn and Leighton, 1946; Vogt, 1961; Young, 1961), yet there are ethnographic accounts of ceremonial assemblies that took up such matters as peace and war prior to the defeat of the Navajo people by Kit Carson in 1846 (Matthews, 1890; Hodge, 1895; Reichard, 1928; Van Valkenburg, 1936, 1946; Brugge, 1963). The large ceremonial assemblies are referred to as *natc'ct* by Reichard (1928, p. 108), who says they throw a "brilliant though slender ray of light on Navajo political organization."

A *natc'ct* or *naach'id* (as used herein) by about 1,000 Navajos, occurred prior to the 1860 attack on Fort Defiance according to Old Nata, an informant of Van Valkenburgh (1946, p. 4). Old Nata's account tells of an assembly that took place near Chinle (near the center of the present Navajo Reservation) when he was in his 12th summer, having been born before 1847. He relates:

> With the falling of the white blossoms of the carrizo my family began to leave their summer camps near the head of Nazlini canyon. Led by my grandfather, who was local headmen, we moved through the forest with the sun. Our travel toward the Chinle valley was slow, for we had to scout ahead for the enemy.
>
> I rode in the middle with the women, old folks and little children.... Ahead of us, behind us, and on our flanks rode the warriors....

Just below Round Rock we again crossed the Chinle Wash traveling east. Long before we reached this place [the location at which Old Nata related this account to Van Valkenburgh] we could see the grey pall of smoke that hung in the sky, for the fires were numerous. And from this knoll upon which we now rest I had my first sight of the assembly.

The flat was covered with people. In the center was a ceremonial hogan partly under the earth. To the east there was a cleared dance ground. Outlining this was a fence of spruce boughs which I later learned had been brought down from the Lukachukai mountains.

As my family went into the encampment we moved to the south side of the hogan. This was according to the tribal status of my grandfather who was one of the 12 Peace Chiefs. Those who followed the 12 War Chiefs were camped on the north side of the ceremonial enclosure.

We soon learned that runners had been sent by the head chief of the tribe to get medicine. He is known to white men by the Mexican name of Sarcillas Largo. [Van Valkenburgh, 1946, pp. 4–5.]

When the runners (six young men and six young girls) returned 4 days later they brought salty mud from the salt lake of Zuni, called *Ashiih* by the Navajo. The salty mud was immediately taken by the young men and women to the central ceremonial hogan and presented to Sarcillas Largo or Nataleeth who served as chief medicine man for the assembly. The six young maidens sat on the north side of the ceremonial hogan with Yaabaa (the Woman that Met the Enemy), and the six young men sat on the south side of the hogan. "Nataleeth led the chant from his seat on the west side of the hogan," relates Old Nata.

Nataleeth opened the assembly on the following day "when the sun reached five fingers above the Tonitsa (Tunica) range." Old Nata states that the 12 war chiefs were seated near the center of the dance ground, and to the south sat the 12 peace chiefs. In between the chiefs was a pile of war gear: bows and arrows; lances with sharp metal points; and shields with pictures of lightning, rainbows, and suns. The war gear meant, Old Nata informs us, that the "assembly had been called for war, for had it been for peace there would have been digging-sticks, carrying baskets and other domestic implements."

Old Nata told how Nataleeth counseled the assembly to follow the path of peace, but that Naba jihlta (Warrior who Grabbed Enemy), later known as Manuelito, jumped up and shouted, "I who was born in four days will lead the Navajo. We will make war and drive these blue-eyed ones from Navajoland." The decision to make war was reached after four days of discussion, and an attack on Fort Defiance was planned. Nataleeth rose to speak, and said:

For four days the War Chiefs led by the eloquent Naba jihlta have been stirring you up to fight these people. Now you have agreed to follow them instead of the Peace Chiefs. With this my power is gone. No longer can I sing Going-to-War songs. For as with many of you—I am going to die! [Ibid., p. 7.]

When Nataleeth finished, he called for his horse and as he rode away Naba jihlta laughed at the prophecy and said to his warriors, *"Ti! Come.* There's a wagon train moving toward Black Rock. After that we will start getting ready to attack Fort Defiance itself." In 1858, nearly 1,000 Navajo warriors attacked the U. S. Army encampment at Fort Defiance and were defeated.

The account by Old Nata of the "last" *naach'id,* the documented report of a tribal assembly held in the vicinity of Canyon de Chelley in 1840 under the leadership of Narbona (Brugge, 1963, pp. 186–187), and the information gathered by Reichard (1928, p. 109), from informants such as Chee Dodge, differ only slightly in details concerning the possibility of counting coup or a related custom at the *naach'id* or general assembly (ibid., p. 111). These reports are highly suggestive of pre-1864 regional political organizations that dealt with problems affecting groups larger than "outfits" (defined by Kluckhohn and Leighton [1946, pp. 62–63] as a group of relatives larger than the extended family who cooperate regularly for certain purposes). The reports of these regional assemblies held prior to 1864 do not indicate whether or not the *naach'id* was a potent force in Navajo life.

We can infer, however, that leaders lacked absolute power for, as Old Nata relates, Nataleeth disassociated himself from the war-minded group and, by leaving the assembly immediately after the decision had been reached to go to war, indicated that he did not abide by this political decision of the war chiefs. We can infer that others who disagreed with the decision suffered only mild negative sanctions, since they followed a venerated leader's example. The patterns of behavior relating to political meetings in the accounts of *naach'id* have their counterparts in contemporary political meetings of Navajos. There are, for example, the long periods of oratory, the attempt to reach consensus, the unwillingness of some to accept the decision of a majority, and the pattern of leave-taking by those who disagree when decisions are reached.

The fragmentary evidence of the *naach'id* indicates a close association between the ceremonial and political life of the Navajo prior to their exile at Fort Sumner in 1864–68, and that perhaps political issues were taken up only when external affairs dictated the need for a political position. The primary functions of the *naach'id* were to cure individuals, to bring rain, and to restore the fertility of the soil (Van Valkenburgh, 1936, p. 18). Whatever place the *naach'id* had in Navajo culture prior to the exile of the majority of Navajo people at Fort

Sumner, there is no evidence that it was revived after the Navajo were released and returned to their homes. However, most major curing ceremonies performed in Navajo country today include speeches by *natani* or leaders—in which the "good life" is urged upon those present—in addition to the conveyance of specific information such as the date of the next grazing committee meeting or ceremonial.

The leadership of local areas prior to the Fort Sumner period was under headmen like Old Nata's grandfather. These men were chosen to direct either the domestic affairs or the war activities of their local group, and no one man could hold both positions. The geopolitical area under their direction was a "natural community" in that it was a self-sufficient ecological unit with boundaries determined by the natural landscape (Hill, 1938, p. 23). The natural community is thought to have contained more than one "outfit," usually three or more to each natural community (Kluckhohn and Leighton, 1946, p. 62).

Both the war and peace chiefs were elected. The choice of a war leader was dependent upon whether or not an individual could perform one or more War Way chants, and the position was open to women as well as men (Hill, 1938, p. 24). The peace chief or *natani* was chosen for his exemplary character, oratorical ability, personal magnetism, proven ability both in religious and practical affairs, and ability to perform the Blessing Way ceremony. Age is not mentioned as a criterion for either position, but the qualifications indicate only older men would normally be eligible.

The people of an area assembled to choose a local headman and, while choice was nearly always unanimous, a close vote would prompt the people to request speeches from the various candidates. In addition, both men and women were allowed to speak in favor of a candidate. The speechmaking and voting frequently took several days; a unanimous vote for one candidate was the objective, as great value was placed upon community solidarity and harmony. The office of headman—either for war or peace—was not considered hereditary, but there was a tendency for a succession to headmanship by the son of a chief, or the chief's sister's son (Hill, 1939, p. 25). Local headmen among the Navajo held office for life; however, a headman was expected to resign before his death and to name a successor. The local group was not bound to accept his recommendation.

The initiation ceremony for a *natani* involved the anointment of his lips with pollen that had been grown on the slopes of the four sacred mountains (Jemez Mountains, Mount Taylor, San Francisco Peaks, and La Plata Mountains) to enable him to make powerful speeches (Wyman and Kluckhohn, 1938, p. 5). The proceedings were accompanied by song, and occasionally tobacco grown on the four sacred peaks was smoked by the candidate (Hill, 1940b, p. 26). After the initiation ritual had been completed, the new *natani* addressed the assembly, asking them to help and obey him. The assembled group normally expressed vocally their willingness to follow the new leader, and at times the group removed their moccasins during the ceremony to indicate their willingness to obey him (Hill, 1940b, p. 26).

The *natani* had to perform his duties by persuasion rather than by force. The success of his administration depended entirely upon his personal magnetism and persuasive ability. His talks were often quite general rather than pointed toward a specific problem, and incorporated such themes as harmony and moderation in all spheres of life, peace, cooperation, and hard work. A *natani* who skillfully wove into his talks stories from the Navajo legends and mythology was accorded high respect both from his own community and from his peers, especially when these talks pointed toward a solution of a current problem.

A *natani* usually appointed several assistants to aid him in overseeing the affairs of the local group. The assistants received no compensation for their work, and neither did the *natani*; their reward was the respect accorded them by the members of their local group. The *natani* was expected to settle domestic quarrels and family disputes and difficulties. In cases involving marital disputes, he called a public meeting in which anyone was allowed to speak. The two major persons in the marital dispute were asked to state their views, and then anyone in the meeting was allowed to contribute information concerning the case. Occasionally, one or both of the involved persons had an older more polished "talker" speak for them and, if the case proved to be difficult, a *natani* asked a member of the community to sum up the evidence given by each side. Regardless of how the case was presented and handled, it was the *natani's* job to settle the dispute. This was accomplished most often by lecturing both parties and asking them to live in peace and harmony and to follow the examples of their grandfathers mentioned in the myths and legends of early Navajo life.

A local headman also judged cases of withcraft and had the right and duty to pronounce sentences of death. Such death sentences had to have the complete approval of the local group and were invoked only in the most serious offenses, and only after long debate and discussion. He was expected to be a generous person, and to dispense hospitality to visitors. A *natani* also represented his local group at large meetings and was the diplomatic representative between his group and other similar groups, tribes, and governments (Hill, 1938, p. 28).

The influence of war chiefs among the Navajo increased toward the middle of the 19th century when raids against the Spanish settlements also increased. It is estimated that the Navajo and Apache took over 450,000 Spanish sheep during the years of 1846 to 1850 (Van

Valkenburgh, 1938, p. 11). Within a month of General Kearny's arrival in Santa Fe in 1846, Navajos stole several head of cattle from General Kearny's beef herd, as well as stealing several thousand head of sheep, goats, and horses from settlers along the Rio Grande near Albuquerque (Vogt, 1961, p. 309).

General Kearny faced the same problem of maintaining peace in the newly acquired Territory that had beset his predecessors for over 100 years. As had the representatives of the Spanish and Mexican governments, he struggled to maintain peace with the various Indian groups in the New Mexico Territory by treaty and by force. In doing so, he repeated most of the errors and fallacies attendant upon previous governments' efforts (Young, 1961, p. 372).

General Kearny (who left the New Mexico Territory in 1846) and his successors apparently were unaware until 1865 that Navajo political organization, along conventional European lines, simply did not exist. Several military expeditions were dispatched against Navajos before 1850, and each returned with signed treaties which pledged them to "Perpetual peace and friendship," and placed them under the jurisdiction of Federal laws (Keleher, 1952, p. 278). In the first (1846) of these treaties concluded between the U.S. Army and the Navajo, Sarcillas Largo or Nataleeth is reputed to have responded:

> Americans, you have a strange cause of war against the Navajos. We have waged war against the New Mexicans for several years. We have plundered their villages and killed many of their people, and made many prisoners. We have a just cause for all this. You have lately commenced a war against the same people. You are powerful. You have great guns and many brave soldiers. You have therefore conquered them, the very thing we have been attempting to do for so many years. You now turn upon us for attempting to do what you have done yourselves. We can not see why you have cause of quarrel with us for fighting the New Mexicans on the west, while you do the same thing on the east. Look how matters stand. This is our war. We have more right to complain of you for interfering in our war than you have to quarrel with us for continuing a war we had begun long before you got here. If you will act justly, you will allow us to settle our own differences. [Vogt, 1961, p. 310.]

Sarcillas Largo and about 500 other Navajos had been rounded up and forced, at bayonet point, to attend the 1846 treaty gathering mentioned above. His arguments failed to sway the Army commander, Colonel Doniphan, and 14 Navajo headmen finally signed a mutual treaty with the Americans. It seems evident, however, that the Navajo leaders thought the Americans were being unjust in their demands, and very possibly would have left the gathering without signing the document if allowed to do so. Conflicts and disputes continued after each treaty, until General Carleton opened a general Indian War in New Mexico in 1863. The raiding career of the Navajo finally ended in 1864, when the majority of them were concentrated at Fort Sumner under close control by the U.S. Army.

Political organization among the Navajo during the first phase of Navajo-American relations (1846–64) had developed to the point where local groups were organized under the dual leadership of peace and war chiefs. These headmen were participants in gatherings or assemblies which attempted to set policies for regional groups of Navajos. It is doubtful, however, that the Navajo ever achieved any effective centralized system of authority even though, during the days when the *naach'id* was held, Navajos were not as widely diffused as they are today. The bulk of the Navajo population during the 1846–64 period was concentrated along the Carrizo, Lukachukai, and Chuska mountains and on the Fort Defiance plateau (Van Valkenburgh, 1936, p. 18).

The local political leaders, the *natani,* operated within a social control system that respected the individual, and uniform collective behavior was achieved not by authoritarian directive imposed from above, but rather by creating a favorable public opinion within the local group. Speeches, debate, and discussion, sometimes all but endless, were consequently the normal means used to create unanimity. The *natani's* status was one of leader and overseer of all of the affairs of his local group or outfit, and he was accorded high rank and prestige. His role was that of a wise leader, and he was expected to combine mythological knowledge with wisdom in making decisions for his group. The reputation of a local headman depended upon his good judgment and his rhetorical ability to persuade members of his group to lead peaceful, useful, and harmonious lives.

Subject People

The Treaty of 1868 between the United States of America and the Navajo Tribe (United States Government, 1946) concluded on June 1, 1868, ratified by Congress on July 25, 1868, and proclaimed by Andrew Johnson, President of the United States, on August 12, 1868, brought to a close General Carleton's attempt to "civilize" the Navajo Indians at Fort Sumner. The Government had spent about two million dollars on the Fort Sumner experiment (Van Valkenburgh, 1938, p. 31), which was to remodel Navajo culture from a semi-nomadic raiding and pastoral way of life to that of a peaceful, settled village-based agricultural way of living, not unlike that practiced in 1860 by the Pueblo people of the Southwest. Yet even a cursory examination of the Treaty of 1868 reveals that the Government was not wholly abandoning its attempts at civilizing the Navajo, and the Government has continued to this day to control certain aspects of the way of life of those Navajos who live within the confines of the Navajo Reservation.

There is little doubt that, to the Navajos at Fort Sumner, the most important feature of the Treaty of 1868 was that they were allowed to return to their homeland, albeit only a small portion of their former territory. The treaty stated that the Navajos were to remain at peace with the United States, and were not to raid other Indian groups, Mexican settlements, or any other groups of people friendly to the Government of the United States. Navajo children were to be sent to school and to be educated ". . . in order to insure the civilization [acculturation] of the Indians . . ." (Treaty of 1868, Art. VI). Navajos were expected to settle upon 160-acre tracts of land and to become farmers. They were expected to stay within the boundaries of the newly created reservation (even though at that time the reservation had not been surveyed), and no person, Indian or White, was to be permitted to enter, reside, or cross the reservation without permission from the agencies directing the affairs of the Navajo. The Treaty of 1868 states that the Government was to issue food, clothing, farming implements, seed, and stock to help the Navajo regain their economic well-being. The U.S. Congress appropriated $150,000 in 1868 to be disbursed for the benefit of the Navajo. One-third of this amount was to be spent on their removal from Fort Sumner and to pay for the costs involved in transporting them to the new reservation. The remaining $100,000 was to be used to purchase cattle, sheep, goats, and corn, which were to be used as rations for the Navajo to tide them over until the first year's crop grown in their own native soil could be harvested. The long hoped for bountiful harvest, however, failed to materialize.

In the fall of 1868 and spring of 1869, the Navajo country suffered from drought. A grasshopper plague added to the bareness of the country, and large game was scarce. There was only a very small number of domesticated stock available to Navajos, and this was principally located far to the northwest among the followers of Hoskinini, who had successfully evaded Kit Carson's troops throughout the Fort Sumner period. In the spring of 1869, seed corn and other seed were distributed to Navajos who came to Fort Defiance, but a late frost and a dry summer destroyed the plants. The Indian Agent and the Navajo felt great discouragement; only by the arrival in November 1869 of the sheep and goats, as promised by the Treaty of 1868, was everyone encouraged (Van Valkenburgh, 1938, p. 36).

Certainly the primary function of the single Indian Agent residing at Fort Defiance was to keep the Navajo from starving; yet he was also expected to make them carry out their promises as stated in the Treaty of 1868. He was held responsible for the behavior of about 9,500 Navajos who were living in scattered hogan settlements in an area of some 3,500,000 acres. In order to carry out his responsibility, the Indian Agent leaned very heavily on several outstanding headmen such as Barboncito,

Manuelito, and Ganado Mucho. The attempts to organize the people into 12 definitive political units during the Fort Sumner period were not continued when the Navajos returned home. Instead, the agent officially recognized Barboncito as the Chief of the Navajo Tribe and held him responsible for his people. In addition, subchiefs were appointed by the Indian Agent on a regional basis. The subchiefs included such leaders as Manuelito, whose home was east of Tohatchi; Ganado Mucho, who lived to the west of the new reservation; Black Horse of Lukachukai, who lived in the north-central section of the reservation; Mariano, who had his camp near Fort Wingate in the eastern section of the reservation; and Hoskinini, who lived far to the northwest near Oljeto. Through these men, the agent was expected to guide and advise the Navajo until they became economically self-sufficient and civilized. The agent was supposed to disburse rations to over 9,000 Navajos, to compel all children between the ages of 6 and 16 to attend school regularly, to help various families select and cultivate 160 acre tracts of land, to give out $10 annually to all who engaged in farming or mechanical pursuits, and to see that peace was maintained between Navajos and Americans. To do this job, the Indian Agent was provided with an office, several clerks and the promise of military assistance if he needed it. In 1869, the Indian Agent moved his office from Fort Wingate to Fort Defiance in order to be more centrally located, even though the latter was not included in the original land assigned to the Navajo as their reservation. Fort Defiance remained the administrative center for all Navajos until 1901, when the reservation was divided up into several distinct administrative units or reservations.

The role of the chiefs during the early years of the Navajo Reservation was to see that peace was maintained between the Navajos and the Americans, and to assist the Indian Agent in his task of promoting well-being and civilization among the Navajo. They were occasionally called into Fort Defiance for "councils," and through these loosely constituted assemblies the agent, via an interpreter, tried to get his program across. The chiefs were then expected to carry the program and ideas out to their respective areas and inform their followers of the agent's decisions and advice. Hoskinini and Black Horse seldom attended these conferences. They were typical of the pre-Fort Sumner kind of leader and did not take easily to the management of their affairs by the Government of the United States (Van Valkenburg, 1936, p. 19). The agent's job was extremely difficult, if not impossible, and, as the older leaders died off, the agents found it necessary to operate in a quasidictatorial manner (Young, 1961, p. 374). This, the Navajo met most frequently with stubborn silence and withdrawal or, very infrequently, countered with acts of violence such as that which occurred at Round Rock in 1892 (Gillmor and Wetherill, 1953, p. 156). The turnover of civil agents at Fort Defiance was rapid; during the period of 1868 to 1900 there were 15 different men appointed as agent for the Navajo, and some only stayed a few months (Underhill, 1953, pp. 275–277).

In the fall of 1869, the promised sheep and goats arrived at Fort Defiance. There were 14,000 sheep and 1,000 goats, which were distributed that winter to 8,121 Navajos (Underhill, 1956, p. 155). Eventually, a total of 30,000 sheep and 4,000 goats were delivered (Van Valkenburgh, 1938, p. 36). Each Navajo was given two animals from the original shipment and the temporary agent, Captain Bennett (1870, p. 148), reported that he had "never seen such anxiety and gratitude."

The reintroduction of sheep and goats among Navajos prompted the reestablishment of a pastoral, transhumant, subsistence pattern, with settlements of scattered, isolated hogan camps. The Navajo territory is one in which those natural resources necessary for maintaining a pastoral way of life occur at scattered locations; locations usually sharply defined by natural barriers (Hill, 1940b, p. 23). In the 1870's, the fundamental political unit among the Navajo was the natural community which still exists in many parts of the area occupied by Navajos today (Levy, 1962, p. 783). The basis for these units is, just as it was in 1868, agricultural land that can be used for pasturage as well as for floodwater-irrigated farm plots. A primary feature of the natural community is one or more natural sources of water both for domestic and for livestock uses.

It was to these "natural communities" that the Navajo returned after their exile at Fort Sumner. These ecologically defined areas contained sociopolitical groups such as the "outfit" and "camp" with the former being the larger, more geographically extensive, and more populous unit. Usually one or more camps made up the sociopolitical unit designated here as the outfit, and the "natural community" normally was the domain of an outfit or, at most, a few outfits (Hill, 1940b, p. 23). The population of these natural communities varied considerably in accordance with the resources available within the ecological unit; while no reliable figures are available, Hill (1940b, p. 23) estimates that the range was from 10 to 40 families.

It is possible to infer, from contemporary accounts and personal observation, that each camp was ordinarily composed of 1 to 10 dwelling units or hogans located adjacent to each other and close enough to be within earshot. A camp formed a "coresidential cooperative unit throughout most of the year" (Collier, 1951, p. 54). Living in each camp there were one or more nuclear families, most often consanguineally related via matrilateral kin. The camp residents today typify an extended family, especially in areas least touched by Anglo-American cultural patterns—e. g., the Navajo Mountain area—and probably represent a traditional familial structure. At present, the extended family within the camp structure can be identified by noting those who habitually eat together.

Information concerning leadership and social organization of Navajo camps is extremely fragmentary for the period prior to 1900. However, in the process of collecting data for the Navajo Tribe, pertaining to their land claims suit against the U.S. Government, it was possible to discern a general pattern for the camp structure after they returned from Fort Sumner in 1868. Almost all of the 300 informants were over 60 years of age, and several had been born before or during the Fort Sumner period. These elder informants, both men and women, indicated that each camp had a spokesman. The spokesman was normally the oldest active male although occasionally a woman might occupy this position. The role of the spokesman was to greet strangers who visited the camp, decide when to move the camp for better pasturage, attend to the affairs external to the camp and thus relate to its members the various events and decisions made by outfit leaders and Government agents.

In like manner, the outfit had a recognized leader, but at times there was more than one leader, especially if the recognized leader was very old and unable to attend to all the affairs of the outfit. The position of an outfit leader was usually held by an older male who had successfully performed one or more Sings and who had the ability to talk persuasively to people, both Navajos and Whites. Superimposed above outfit leaders were such men as Manuelito, Ganado, Mucho, and Mariano, who were recognized as leaders of several geographically contiguous outfits, described above as natural communities. The leaders of these natural communities were recognized by the Indian Agents as chiefs and subchiefs of the Navajo tribe. In summary fashion, Young states:

> The extended family group, is an aspect of a larger, although more loosely associated, sociological unit, commonly referred to as a community. There are no communities in the sense of being villages in the Navajo country except as such have grown up around Government schools, hospitals and administrative centers or around missions. Towns or villages are not aspects of Navajo culture itself. However, under the leadership of one or more of the ablest family heads, families and family groups cooperate as members of a community group, tied by bonds of marriage, relationship, adjacent residence, common interest and the like. The community groups can be closely identified with specific areas of land use and residence, and each has its own social structure. They are not formalized nor closely knit units, but they are basic to traditional land use and economy on the Reservation. [Young, 1961, p. 369.]

The land-use community or natural community as a distinct, politically independent unit was reinforced in these key areas from 1869 until about 1950 by the establishment of missions, schools, trading posts, and such units as grazing cooperatives and chapters in the 1920's and 1930's (Hill, 1940b, p. 24).

The Governmental programs, such as schools for Navajo children, while successful in one area, met fierce resistance in another. Some of the leaders of these natural communities strongly objected to any intrusions by the Government agents, White trappers, missionaries, or White cattlemen. The attitude toward White intrusion and the feeling of independence present among Navajos is attested to by several outbreaks of armed resistance against Governmental directives and policies. Among the best known of these acts of violence is that which occurred in 1892 at Round Rock, which was in the land use community guided by Black Horse. This powerful leader was very much opposed to children being taken away and placed in the school at Fort Defiance. When Black Horse heard that the Indian Agent Dana Shipley was on his way to collect children from his area, he gathered together some of his band and met with Shipley at Round Rock in an attempt to dissuade him. The agent listened to Black Horse's arguments, but insisted on taking about 30 or 40 children back to Fort Defiance to place them in school. Black Horse, with the help of his band, then attacked Shipley and the Navajo policemen with him.

An account of the fracas is given by Left-Handed Mexican Clansman, who was present (for he was willing to go with Agent Shipley to attend the Fort Defiance school) during the 3-day ordeal (Young and Morgan, 1952, pp. 23–31). Left-Handed Mexican Clansman recalls that he and a companion persuaded their parents to let them join the other young people gathering at the trading post, located at Blue Clay Point, owned jointly by Chee Dodge and S. E. Aldrich of Manuelito, New Mexico, and:

> When we got to the store we found that many people had assembled. Many horses were standing about. At that time horses were the only means people had for transportation. Some of us did not know what had been done the night before. All we had found out was that someone by the name of Black Horse had brought a party from the other side of the mountain.
>
> We were told that now there would be work here making out papers for more of our children. There were three Navajo policemen there in that connection. One of them turned out to be Bead Clan Gambler, one was Singed Man from Fort Defiance—he was also known as Son of Former Rag Man. Another was Interpreter's (i.e., Chee Dodge's) brother-in-law, a Red Streak Into Water Clansman. . . . So there were the three policemen. It happened that way. . . . We saw the people going inside the trading post, so we just went in with

the crowd. We two who were going to school stayed together. As for the rest of the children who were going to school, I don't know anything about them.

The people went into the trading post. It was packed full. Over here on one side the counter ran. Further back in the room was a swinging gate. It was out through there that Chee came. . . . A little later the one called Little Chief (Shipley) came out and stopped beside Chee. Chee was his interpreter as he began to make a speech to the people. Black Horse was standing against the counter over to one side. The people of his band were standing with him. The people who had promised their children for school were named, and we were told many things about the school.

Then Black Horse spoke up and said, "This business of taking children away from people to put them in school—when is it going to affect the people from over beyond the mountain."

"It will reach you sometime. Tomorrow these will start out, and will be routed right along the mountainside," said Little Chief (Shipley).

"We'll not give you a one of our children. And we'd just as soon fight over this matter as not," said Black Horse balking stubbornly.

Speaking this way to each other the Agent and Black Horse exchanged many words.

"Come on, you boys. Remember what you said," said Black Horse.

The one called Limper was the first to hop in there, and he grabbed the Agent by the collar. Then they all rushed in. Chee jumped over the gate at the back of the room, and chaos followed.

"Outside with him!" voices were saying

They started out with him. As they were taking him outside I crawled and squeezed myself out among them. Just then they locked the door from the inside. . . .

The mob was carrying the Agent away. Not far from there, there was a drop. There was a wash in the blue clay with a point of land on either side. That is how the trading post got its name. It was a long drop.

"Throw him down there!" voices were heard saying.

A lot of people were standing alongside the trading post, and I among them. . . . As the people carried the Agent along they beat him with their fists. They were beating him up. But as they carried him further away the one called Bead Clan Gambler went running from here where we were standing.

"What the devil are you trying to do, boys?" he said as he went running into the mob, shoving people backwards.

The man whose son had been locked in the trading post ran in there with him. And a number of his friends in turn followed him into the mob. They rescued the Agent. (Ibid., pp. 26–27.)

Left-Handed Mexican Clansman finishes his narrative by explaining that one of the policemen escaped and brought U.S. Army troops back to Round Rock some 36 hours later and rescued the Fort Defiance party which had barricaded themselves in the trading post; thus peace was restored (ibid., p. 30).

Agent Shipley attempted to have Black Horse captured and brought before a tribunal but, for reasons unknown, the U.S. Army never acted upon his repeated requests for punitive action against Black Horse and his followers.

About a month after the trouble at Round Rock, Agent Shipley called a meeting of headmen to discuss the difficulties at Round Rock, and to formulate a plan of action to be taken against Black Horse. The meeting was held on November 25, 1892, at Fort Defiance, but Black Horse and the Round Rock affair were scarcely mentioned. Instead, the headmen spent most of their time complaining about the treatment of their children at the Fort Defiance school. The complaints specifically mentioned Mr. Wadleigh, the school superintendent (ibid., p. 11).

When we put our children in school it was like giving our hearts up, and when the Superintendent abuses our children it hurts us very much. The name we have given this superintendent is Billy Goat. A billy goat is always butting all the rest of the sheep and imposing on them, and we think this is a good name for him. We make this complaint to you white people who want to see children well treated. And now we want a new superintendent who will take interest in our children and treat them as we do.

Early in 1893, Agent Shipley and Mr. Wadleigh resigned, and the new Indian Agent appointed was Lieut. Edwin H. Plummer.

Lieutenant Plummer, who remained Indian Agent for the Navajo for 4 years, became convinced early in his tenure that many of the younger people believed that the Navajo far outnumbered the Whites and could easily overpower the Whites and regain full independence. Being a man of direct action, Agent Plummer took a number of younger Navajos to the World's Colombian Exposition in Chicago, Ill., in 1893 (ibid., p. 19). It was Agent Plummer's belief that Indians learn and are influenced almost entirely by observation; he therefore recommended that a carload of Navajo Indians visit Washington, two or three larger cities, and Vassar College, for the purpose of seeing something of the educational methods of Americans, in the hope that they would realize the power, extent, and advantages of the American way of life. His plan was to select many of the young men of the Navajo Tribe; the majority to be from regions farthest from the administrative centers of the reservation, and from the ranks of those most opposed to adopting civilized modes of living and the educational advantages offered for their children.

When the travelers returned, they told Agent Plummer (Young and Morgan, 1952, p. 20):

> They had always supposed that they knew all about the country we were traveling through from their ancestors, but that they now saw that they were mistaken. They had supposed that there were very few white men in that part of the country, but they saw that it was full of them, . . . (and that) when the other Navajos were "acting mean" he had something to tell them that would make them behave themselves.

These two events and methods produced quite different results. Agent Shipley's techniques resulted in armed resistance while, under Agent Plummer's guiding hand, interest in education began to grow in 1893 and schools became overcrowded. The methods employed by Agent Plummer reduced resistance to schooling for Navajo children and, in 1894, 16 children were brought in from the Round Rock neighborhood by Navajo parents.

The glimpses of Navajo leadership presented by these accounts are illuminating. The most dramatic feature is observable in the behavior of Black Horse who had organized a means not only to prevent the Indian Agent taking away Navajo children for schooling but also to assert his position as the supreme authority in that particular region. Black Horse's leadership was supported by other headmen of the area in later meetings with the Indian Agent, as well as by the U.S. Army personnel which failed to respond to Agent Shipley's demand that Black Horse be brought in for his acts of defiance. The Navajo headmen called in by Agent Shipley to discuss Black Horse's action ignored his request to "hold court" on Black Horse, but instead criticized Agent Shipley's handling of the school at Fort Defiance. In ignoring the Black Horse condemnation desired by Agent Shipley, the headmen supported the action and leadership of Black Horse and eventually paved the way for a new agent to be appointed for the Navajo.

Agent Plummer's methods incorporated recognizing regional leaders as well as educating recalcitrant members of the Navajo Tribe via direct observation of the things a school education brought. In addition, Agent Plummer attempted to enlist Black Horse's aid in settling disputes between Navajos and Whites along the San Juan River, for as Agent Plummer states ". . . it is as a chief on whom I must depend to help me control the Navajos . . ." (ibid., p. 13).

It is to Agent Plummer's credit that he saw clearly his problem of controlling the Navajo; he saw that he could not deal effectively with the opposition to change unless he had the support and aid of a chief of the people. To me, it appears that Plummer saw and understood clearly that the U.S. Government was imposing patterns of behavior upon the Navajo that were foreign to them. Thus, he needed a Navajo leader who would be able to convince more traditional Navajos to accept the new order of things introduced by the Indian Agent. Chiefs of the Navajo Tribe up to Agent Plummer's time, and later, were creations of the U.S. Government, and as such did not enjoy tribal-wide support, as the Navajo looked to their headmen, outfit, and community leaders for direction. The traditional pattern of social control among Navajos respects the individual; uniform collective behavior is achieved by publicly imposing mild sanctions (gossip and ridicule) against those who deviate too far from the norm, and not by authoritarian directives from persons in positions of leadership. A headman is expected to provide wise counsel, and his reputation as a leader rests upon his good judgment as well as upon his eloquence in presenting his advice (Franciscan Fathers, 1910, p. 422). In terms of the traditional Navajo culture, the socially acceptable means to achieve uniform collective behavior was to talk and to discuss the issue until all were convinced (or too embarrassed to raise further objections) and thereby achieve consensus.

Beginning with the Fort Sumner period of control of the Navajo, the Government had placed certain "natural" leaders in official positions of leadership for the entire tribe. Headmen and outfit leaders had little choice but to accept these positions; they then acted out the official roles defined by the Indian Agents. There remained untouched, however, many informal leaders such as camp spokesmen. These informal leaders resented interference from the outside in matters concerning the life practiced by their followers, whether it came from Indian Agents or other Navajos.

The Indian Agent's job had become increasingly complex by 1890, due in part to increases in Navajo population. It is estimated that there were 9,000–10,000 Navajos in 1868, and in 1880 the number had increased to 15,500. By 1910, there were approximately 22,455 people; and thereafter a steady increase took place until in 1960 about 93,000 Navajos resided in Navajo country (Young, 1961, p. 147). The agents during this entire period had to face the problem of expanding grazing resources for stock to accommodate the growing Navajo population; although new lands were added periodically by Executive Order extension or Act of Congress, the new land did not keep pace with the requirements for living and grazing space needed by the expanding population. By 1880, the reservation lands totaled 6,750,000 acres, with an additional 6,000,000 acres of nonreservation land that was used by Indians (Van Valkenburgh, 1938, p. 48). In the 1880's the Navajo enjoyed a period of comparative prosperity. Some had become wealthy, counting their herds by the hundreds.

The Indian Agent for all Navajos was located at Fort Defiance until 1901, and to assist him were a clerk, a physician, a farmer, a herdsman, a chief of scouts, and a school teacher; the agency also had three horses to use in official travel (Van Valkenburgh, 1938, p. 48). It is easy to understand why most Navajos were unimpressed with the White men guiding their affairs during the latter part of the 19th century and the first part of the 20th century.

The increased land area of the Navajo Reservation, the increased population and relative prosperity of the Navajo (map 3), plus the establishment of trading posts and missions in various natural communities in key regional areas served to dilute the influence of the single Indian Agent. The agent stationed at Fort Defiance was able to make contact personally with only a small minority of the Navajo, most of whom lived close to Fort Defiance.

Some Navajo leaders became known for the way they "talked back" to the agent, and other Navajos became known for their ability to present the Indian Agent with the Navajo point of view in English. The former type of leader is typified by Peshlakai of Crystal, who was frequently chosen as a spokesman for the Navajo since they liked to hear the silversmith "tell off" the Government people in his bluff and laconic way. Peshlakai is described as one who could make the White Government officials wince and the Navajos laugh, and as a leader who sensed the bitter hatred his people had against the Government practice of sending the children off the reservation to boarding schools (Wilken, 1955, p. 176). This informal leader is reported to have said, "You drive all over our land in your yellow wagons to take away our healthy children; then you drop them off at Gallup as bags of skin and bones when you are through with them" (Weber, et al., 1908, pp. 36–37).

The second kind of leader—the kind who could interpret and convey in English to the Indian Agent, the wants,

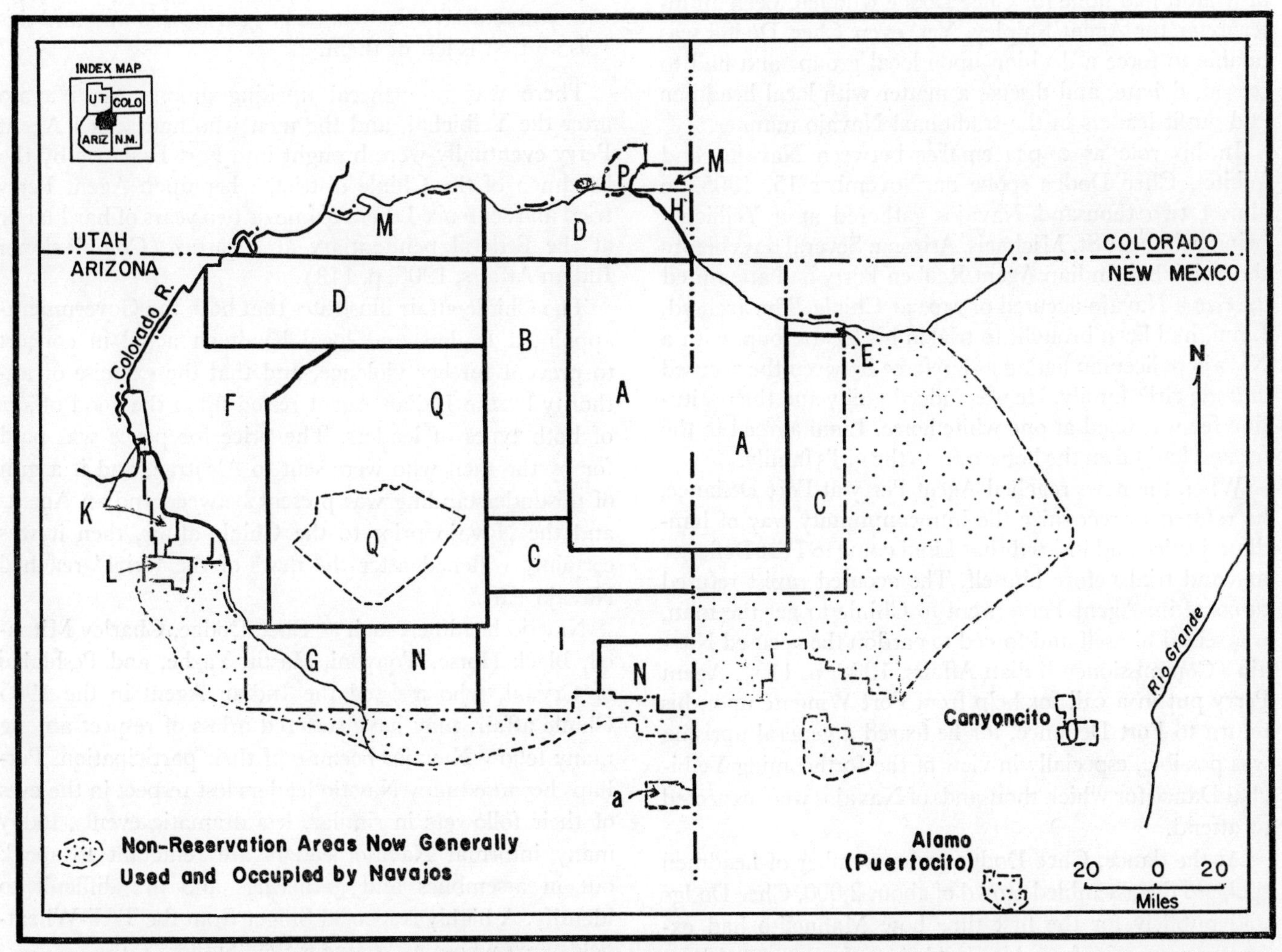

Map 3.—Expansion of the Navajo Reservation, 1868–1962. *A*, Treaty of June 1868. *B*, Executive Order of Oct. 29, 1878. *C*, Exec. Order Jan. 6, 1880. *D*, Exec. Order May 17, 1884. *E*, Exec. Order April 24, 1886. *F*, Exec. Order Jan. 8, 1900. *G*, Exec. Order Nov. 14, 1901. *H*, Exec. Order May 15, 1905. *I*, Exec. Order Nov. 7. 1907. *J*, Exec. Order May 7, 1917. *K*, Act of May 23, 1930. *L*, Act of Feb. 21, 1931. *M*, Act of March 1, 1933. *N*, Act of June 14, 1933. *O*, Act of Aug. 13, 1949. *P*, Act of Sept. 2, 1958. *Q*, District Court Judgment of Sept. 28, 1962. *a*, Bar-N Ranch, owned by the Navajo Tribe. (U.S.G.S., State, and Navajo Tribe Land Investigation Division maps.)

desires, and needs of the Navajo—began to enjoy greater prestige after 1890. An outstanding example was Chee Dodge. Chee Dodge gained a reputation among his fellow Navajos for being able to negotiate and talk to White men, and was held in high regard by many Navajos and Whites for his persuasive abilities. Other Navajo men who signed on as agency policemen enjoyed a certain amount of respect in their own regions, as did the men who worked as interpreters for missionaries and traders. These men who had official, wage paying jobs with non-Navajo agencies were often called upon to speak at large gatherings—such as Yeibichai Dances and other Sings—which marked them as persons of considerable rank and high prestige and, at the same time, distinguished them as "outsiders" and different from Navajos who were leading a traditional Navajo way of life. Left-Handed Mexican Clansman, the narrator of the Round Rock-Black Horse affair, was prompted to seek a school education in view of what it had done for Chee Dodge who had been an interpreter for Agent Shipley. Yet, even Chee Dodge was unable to force a decision upon local groups and had to reason, debate, and discuss a matter with local headmen and outfit leaders in the traditional Navajo manner.

In his role as a peacemaker between Navajos and Whites, Chee Dodge spoke on November 15, 1905, to almost two thousand Navajos gathered at a Yeibichai being held near St. Michaels, Arizona. Several days before the Yeibichai, Indian Agent Reuben Perry had attempted to seize a Navajo accused of rape at Chinle. The accused, Linni, had been brought to trial in his local group, with a Navajo policeman acting as a referee between the accused and the girl's family. He was judged guilty and the restitution fee was fixed at one white horse. Linni agreed to the fee and had taken the horse over to the girl's family.

When the news reached Agent Perry at Fort Defiance, he refused to recognize the intracommunity way of handling justice and insisted that Linni come to Fort Defiance to stand trial before himself. The accused rapist refused to come in. Agent Perry went to Chinle to get the man, was seized himself and forced to pardon the accused Navajo (Commissioner Indian Affairs, 1906, p. 115). Agent Perry put in a call for help from Fort Wingate upon his return to Fort Defiance, for he feared a general uprising was possible, especially in view of the forthcoming Yeibichai Dance for which thousands of Navajos were expected to attend.

At the dance, Chee Dodge and a number of headmen spoke to the assembled crowd of about 2,000. Chee Dodge told publicly for the first time how Manuelito had extracted a promise from him just before the venerated War Chief had died; Chee had promised Manuelito to lead the Navajo along the path of peace, so that they would not destroy themselves by trying to fight the Government (Wilken, 1955, p. 175). The *McKinley County Republican* published a portion of Chee's talk on December 16, 1905:

> The President has given you a long rope so you may graze wherever you please. If a man has a good horse and pickets him out he gives him a long rope in good grass and lets him graze as far as he can; but if he has a mean horse he gives him a short rope with his head tied close to a post so he can get but little feed. The President has given you a long rope. Some of you have a very long rope; you live very far from the Reservation; others who live nearer the Reservation have a shorter rope; but the President has a rope on every one of you, and if you do not appreciate the good treatment you are given, if you try to make trouble, he will pull on all the ropes and draw you fellows all together to a tight place. . . . You will lose your stock, and you will be afoot, you will be nothing, you will be wiped out, and you will be guarded by troops, and everybody will laugh at you and say "See what a large tribe this was, and this is all that is left of them."

There was no general uprising among the Navajo after the Yeibichai, and the men who had seized Agent Perry eventually were brought into Fort Defiance by the headmen of the Chinle district, whereupon Agent Perry tried and sentenced them to one or two years of hard labor at the Federal penitentiary at Alcatraz (Commissioner Indian Affairs, 1906, p. 118).

The Chinle affair illustrates that both the Government-appointed leaders and local headmen acted in concert to prevent further violence, and that the exercise of authority by the Indian Agent rested upon the good offices of both types of leaders. The price for peace was paid for by the men who were sent to Alcatraz, and if a gulf of misunderstanding was present between Indian Agents and the Navajo prior to the Chinle affair, then it was certainly widened after the news of the "trial" reached Navajo ears.

Navajo headmen such as Chee Dodge, Charley Mitchell, Black Horse, Tqayoni, Hastin Yazhe, and Peshlakai of Crystal, who assisted the Indian Agent in the 1905 Chinle affair, may have suffered a loss of respect among many fellow Navajos because of their participation. Perhaps because many Navajo leaders lost respect in the eyes of their followers in similar, less dramatic events, today many informal Navajo leaders are reluctant to speak out in assemblies and gatherings and are difficult to identify. A highly respected Singer from the Tseli-Wheatfields area whose nickname is the "Smiler" said:

> I used to be president of the chapter but after several terms, I got tired of people blaming me for everything that happened here. I got tired of protecting myself and my family from [supernatural] arrows, so I let

other men do it now . . . if people want my advice they know where they can find me.

Whatever the case may have been in the early years of the 20th century, a division appears to have occurred between the informal and the formal Navajo leaders, a rift which has continued to widen until recently. However, Chee Dodge kept a foot in both camps, and was respected both by Navajos and Whites, even after his death in 1948.

The political structure created by the Government for the Navajo failed to incorporate the leaders on the local levels during the period from 1868 to 1936. In 1936 the reservation was canvassed for the purpose of identifying the Navajo leadership in the persons of the most influential headmen, who were to be asked to serve as members of a constitutional assembly (Young, 1961, p. 379). As mentioned above, the sociopolitical distance between the local leaders and the leaders appointed by the Government widened after 1900. This separation was partially due to: (1) an increase in demands by the Indian Agent that Navajos obey the regulations and laws passed by the U.S. Congress; (2) the arbitrary manner in which many of the Indian Agents governed the Navajo, especially in regard to the punishment imposed upon Navajos when they were tried before the Indian Agent; and (3) the regional isolation of many Navajos who lived hundreds of miles from the administrative centers. In addition, the Government-appointed Navajo leaders, while frequently looked upon by fellow Navajos with awe and a measure of respect, were seldom imitated (Underhill, 1956, p. 210). These Government-appointed leaders sought to bring about changes in the traditional Navajo culture that would accommodate Navajos to the social and political conditions imposed upon them by the Government. In behaving thus, the Government-appointed leaders were threats to the security of those who lived in the traditional Navajo way. Conceptually, such leaders as Chee Dodge, Barboncito, Ganado Mucho, and Manuelito (after 1868), assumed positions of leadership that were in opposition to the traditional Navajo pattern of leadership, which has its focal point on the local level.

Utilizing Godfrey and Monica Wilson's concept of radical and ordinary opposition within a broader framework of a functional integration of elements and traits within a social system, it is possible to isolate the structural positions and functions of each type of leader in Navajo society (Wilson and Wilson, 1945, p. 23). Opposition, according to the Wilsons, has two forms: ordinary and radical (ibid., p. 125). Ordinary opposition occurs in all social systems and relates to the normal disputes and frictions within a social group over who is to assume preexisting social positions, how the existing rules of conduct are to be applied, and who is to have power over another within conventional culturally defined limits.

Among the Navajos of 1900, ordinary opposition was resolved when a new person had been chosen subsequent to the death of a local leader. The procedure prescribed and generally followed until about 1920 for the election of a new leader for a Navajo local group included a waiting period of 1 to 3 months after the death of a leader, an assembly of all adult Navajos within the area, talks to the assembled group by several camp spokesmen concerning whom they favored, and a vote by the assembly for the various candidates. The voting procedure was accomplished by adults walking over to, and placing themselves behind, the candidate of their choice. In the event an election vote divided the local group, the candidates would be asked to speak and exhibit their skill at talking persuasively. Another "vote" was taken, and if still the group remained divided, additional speeches would be made by candidates and their sponsers until a consensus was reached. In the event that a consensus was not reached in several days, the group was dissolved with an understanding that there was to be another meeting at a later date, generally within the next 6 months. During the period that the local group was without a leader, the people discussed the qualifications of each possible candidate. These discussions were conducted on an informal basis at camps, trading posts, Sings, Yeibichai Dances, and dipping vats for stock; by the time the local group convened, the number of candidates was normally only two or three.

Both men and women spoke at these local assemblies; the meeting was guided by a respected man, at times an outsider such as a leader of an adjacent local group, and the tenor of the deliberations was informal. Individuals sat or stood in a semicircle around the main speakers during the meeting, and movement in and out of the main body of the assembled group was not considered disrespectful. In general, the men sat together and not with their spouses, and the children were considered the responsibility of the women. Older men and women did most of the talking, and they were given greater attention and respect when they spoke than were the younger people. Respect generally was shown in two ways: the first was to remain silent during a person's talk; the second was for the speaker following a highly respected man or woman to repeat portions of the former speaker's talk, to indicate how carefully he had followed the speech. This process of selecting a local leader among Navajos was democratic; since the choice of leaders was not by a simple majority but by a consensus, it was integrated within the Navajo value system which stresses harmony. The methods used by the Navajos prior to the 1920's did not result in disequilibrium within the social system; rather, the selection of leaders by consensus functioned to reinforce the existing social structure. Not only was there unanimous agreement on who was to be a leader, but he dared not act as an autocrat lest he either be accused of being a witch or have witchcraft directed against him or members of his family

(Kluckhohn and Leighton, 1946, p. 178). An elder informant from Wheatfields described such a leader in the following manner:

> A *natani* in the days before the council was always seen on the same horse, and he talked to the people from horseback. [Why did he ride the same horse all the time?] A *natani* always rode the same horse to show the people that he was not afraid of witchcraft, and he let the horse go (defecate) just any place and would let it just lie there and never bother to scoop it up. [How does horse manure relate to his position of leadership?] It has everything to do with it. A leader was showing his disregard for witchcraft, and anyone who wanted to try and harm him was free to try by using the horse manure, but the fact that the leader always rode the same horse showed that he was capable of warding-off any witchcraft practiced against him, and in this way he indicated he was a strong healthy leader.

The same informant stated that if a leader's horse should die suddenly, or several sheep die unexpectedly, or a member of his family get sick, he would have to have one or more ceremonials to restore balance and harmony in his life. Under such conditions a leader would temporarily disengage himself from the position of leadership and resume it only after the ceremonies had been completed. In the event that a leader was plagued with a series of misfortunes, he would withdraw completely from the position of leadership and allow another to assume the position of political leader.

The Government-sponsored leaders of the Navajo people, all of whom were appointed to their positions by agents of the Government, were not supported by a popular vote in their positions as leaders. However, the earlier men, such as Barboncito, Manuelito, and Ganado Mucho who were appointed to these offices by the Government, had been "natural" leaders in their respective areas; men like Chee Dodge were selected for formal positions of leadership by the Indian Agent primarily because of their ability to speak both English and Navajo as well as their cooperative attitude toward remodeling Navajo culture along lines that were prescribed by the Government. In terms of this conceptual scheme, borrowed from the Wilsons (1945), Government-appointed leaders for the Navajo are in social positions that radically oppose the indigenous Navajo social structure.

Radical opposition is different from ordinary opposition in that it cannot be resolved within the preexisting cultural patterns. Radical opposition affects every social position, every rule and regular behavior pattern of a group, and it is in opposition to the preexisting social structure itself and to what that structure is to become (Wilson and Wilson, 1945, p. 125). The Navajo men who were appointed to positions of leadership by the Government could only be incorporated into a Navajo social system after it had changed and new positions were created for them to occupy. There were no "appointed" leadership positions within the traditional Navajo culture; men assumed leadership by the consent of the people they were going to lead. Thus, there were no preexisting social positions for Government-appointed leaders to assume, and the whole traditional Navajo social system had to undergo changes to accommodate the demands of the Government. The Navajo repeatedly rejected foreign political controls that were imposed upon them—first by the Spanish, then by the Mexicans, and then by the Americans—until they were defeated by an American military force in 1863 and were subsequently made a people subject to the U.S. Government. Thus, the Navajo, under military threat, were forced to accept a new form of leadership which was inconsistent with the traditional Navajo culture.

The function of a leader within the traditional Navajo culture is thereby opposed to the formal leaders, yet these opposed social positions are not normally recognized in cultures undergoing social change: "for it to be generally, i.e. consistently, realized in action, concept, and expression is for it to be overcome" (loc. cit.).

Such a leader as Chee Dodge maintained loyalties, habits, contacts, influence, and affections with the traditional Navajos as well as, at times, participating in cultural patterns that originated with the Anglo-American society. Chee Dodge was able to perform Sings, speak fluent Navajo, recite Navajo mythical tales and recognize signs of witchcraft, yet he also had a bank account, a modern house, spoke English, sent his children to college, and amassed a fortune which he willed to his children. The informal, local leaders achieved their position of leadership by virtue of being selected by their groups as leaders. The characteristics of such informal leaders are and were that they should be able to exhibit a modest amount of wealth, that they be mature, male, and have the knowledge and ability to perform one or more Sings. Frequently these informal leaders are found to wear their hair long in a bun at the back and to wear several pieces of turquoise in the forms of a necklace, on a hatband, as a belt buckle, or as buttons to clasp their deerskin moccasins. In addition, the informal leaders are usually members of the most populous clan in their area or region. Almost invariably these local leaders have lived in the same region or locality all of their lives, and only a very few speak a non-Navajo language.

In contrast, the formal or appointed leaders of the Navajo Tribe from 1868 to 1923, when a tribal council was organized with Chee Dodge as the first Chairman, frequently spoke a non-Navajo language (English and/or Spanish) and lived in locations other than the place of their birth and early childhood. The Government-appointed leaders often received wages for performing services for the Government agents and were appointed, not elected, to their positions of leadership. Both types of leaders had many characteristics in common: both were Navajo, spoke Navajo, were older males, and frequently had reputations as persuasive speakers and a knowledge of the mythical creation of the Navajo people.

The "council" held in 1922 (see p. 19) was composed of Chee Dodge, Charley Mitchell, and Daaghaa'Chii Bikiis, and considered the leasing of tribal land for oil exploration (Van Valkenburgh, 1938, p. 55). However, until the formation of a Tribal Council in 1923, prompted by an assembly held on January 22, 1922, at Fort Defiance, the Navajo had no choice in the selection of their formal leaders. Thus, in 1923 began a new era as the Navajo gained the opportunity to choose who would represent them on a tribal-wide basis.

Beginnings in Tribal Self-Government

NAVAJO TRIBAL COUNCIL

The administrative units into which contemporary Navajos have been organized by the Government had their beginning with the Treaty of 1868, when a three and one-half million acres tract of land was set aside for the Navajo in the north central area of the New Mexico Territory. Under this treaty, the Navajo became subject to the authority of the United States and their lives were to be guided by agents of the Government, a status they still retain. Each of the administrative units has its own history of development and function within contemporary Navajo culture, and while the position is taken here that each aspect of a cultural system is functionally related to every other aspect, a selection has been made to discuss only those sociopolitical units that have led to greater self-government among the Navajo. Our attention will be focused on the Navajo Tribal Council, chapters, and the grazing committees; currently the membership of these units is elective. A 1962 list of contemporary Navajo sociopolitical units that have been the result of action by the Government includes: 19 land management districts; 66 grazing committees; 34 grazing community organizations; 1 Bureau of Indian Affairs area office; 2 Bureau of Indian Affairs agency offices; 5 Bureau of Indian Affairs subagencies; 10 counties in 4 States; 71 school districts; 96 chapter organizations; 74 Navajo Tribal Council districts; 4 provincial election districts; and 19 district tribal councils.

In a general way, Navajo people can be divided into two groups: those living on the Navajo Reservation, and those living off the reservation. Our discussion will include both groups, limiting the second to those Navajos living within 100 miles of the reservation. There is one exception to this limitation (see p. 24).

A single administrative center located first at Fort Wingate (Underhill, 1956, p. 150), then shortly later at Fort Defiance, Arizona, guided the affairs of the Navajo from 1868 to 1901 (Young, 1961, p. 373). Beginning with the year 1901, the Navajo country was divided into separate agency jurisdictions (map 4), and by 1934 a total of six had been created (including the Moqui Agency, which served both Navajo and Hopi) (Young, 1961, p. 374). In 1934, five of these were combined (Moqui Agency excluded) under a single administrative agency with headquarters at Window Rock, Arizona. The combined jurisdictions included: San Juan Agency (later Shiprock); Pueblo Bonito Agency (later Crownpoint); Southern Navajo Agency (later Fort Defiance); Western Navajo Agency (later Tuba City); and the Leupp Agency (later incorporated with Tuba City).

The division of Navajo country into six separate agency jurisdictions (map 5) in the period from 1901 to 1934, reduced the expanse of territory for which each superintendent was responsible. Aside from bringing the Indian Agents physically closer to more Navajo Indians, however, it accomplished very little else, especially in the realm of self-government for Navajos. The separate agency administrative structures did not function positively in fostering tribal unity, and they did not promote any form of tribal government. However, older Navajo informants occasionally express a longing "for the good old days" when they could take their troubles to an agency superintendent and get a direct answer. When these informants are questioned concerning to what period they refer, they state, "Before the Flu epidemic [1917–18], when we had our own superintendent." Today, the pattern persists in that much of the tribal chairman's time

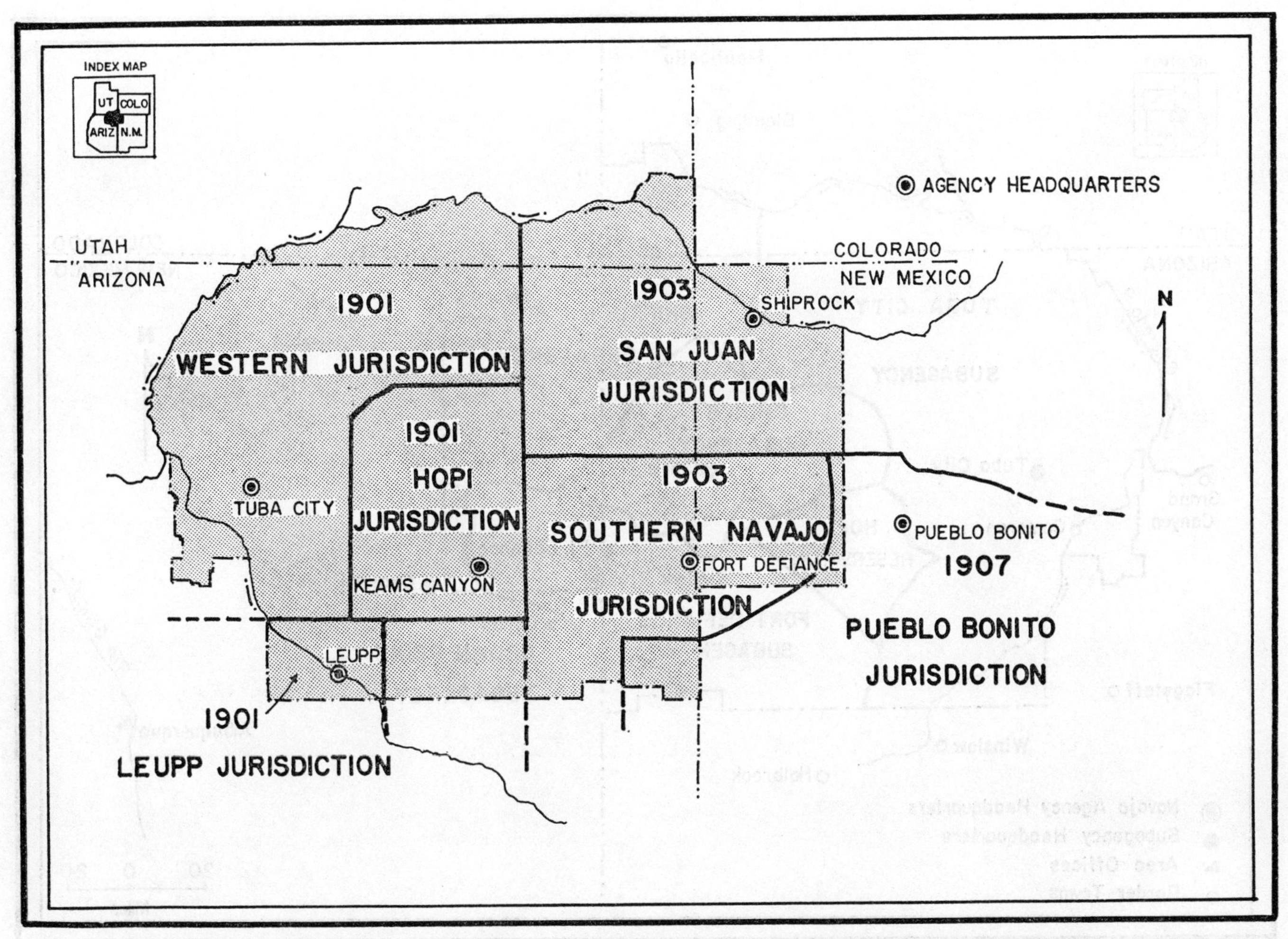

MAP 4.—Navajo jurisdictions, 1901–35. (U.S.G.S., State, and Navajo Tribe Land Investigation Division maps.)

is spent listening to requests from older men and women who prefer to present their complaint or request to him rather than to a tribal bureaucrat or an agency official. Even with the Government's extension of its paternalistic role by creating six agency superintendents to work with the Navajo and their problems, it was in this period (1901–34) that the Government first allowed the Navajo to select by popular vote their own leaders to represent them on a tribal-wide basis.

The first concrete steps made by the Government toward allowing the Navajo a measure of self-government occurred in 1923, when the first tribal council was elected.[4] It has been mentioned above that occasionally Indian Agents had called in headmen and outfit leaders for a council, and these hand-picked assemblies were expected to act on behalf of all of the Navajo. It is very possible that the Indian Agents operating on the local levels recognized the inadequacy of these "councils" and that a more representative form of government for the Navajo was not only possible, but needed. Yet it was not until oil was discovered, on land originally set aside by the Treaty of 1868, that the need was sufficiently compelling to overcome the inertia that had previously prevented the establishment of a representative tribal government (Young, 1961, p. 374). Article X of the Treaty of 1868 provided:

> No future treaty for the cession of any portion or part of the reservation herein described, which may be held in common, shall be of any validity or force against said Indians unless agreed to and executed by at least three-fourths of all the adult male Indians occupying or interested in the same. . . . [Navajo Tribal Code, 1962, p. 288]

In 1921, the Navajos of the San Juan jurisdiction, acted in accordance with this Article and voted to lease a 4,800 acre tract of land to the Midwest Refining Company. Although the use of a general assembly of Navajos within a jurisdiction was a clumsy and time-consuming method for conducting business, several oil leases were negotiated by Navajos of several jurisdictions

[4] In 1903, a Court of Indian Offenses was established. Although the court included three Indian judges, appointed by the Agency Superintendent, the Superintendent presided at all hearings and decisions (Underhill, 1956, p. 220).

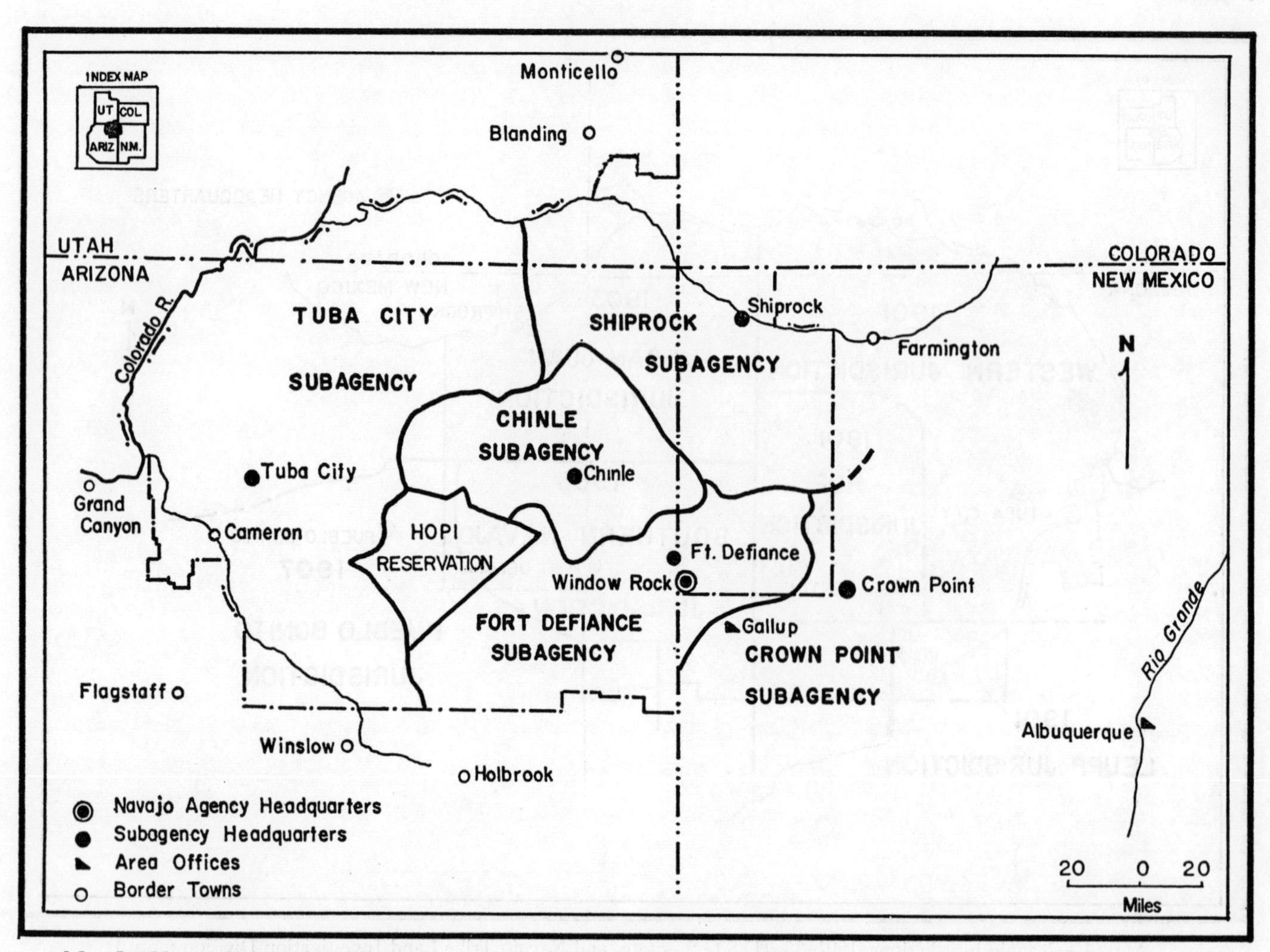

Map 5.—Navajo Reservation subagencies, 1935–61. (U.S.G.S., State, and Navajo Tribe Land Investigation Division maps.)

in 1921, only to meet with disapproval and veto by the Secretary of the Interior. In these negotiations, the Navajos were exercising the rights of franchise given them by the Treaty of 1868. The departmental reason for the disapproval of the leases was that the land in question was originally set aside for all the Navajo people, and that the revenue that might come from such land belonged to all of the Navajos, not only those living in this or that particular jurisdiction.

In short, the policy of the Department of the Interior was that any reservation land with its resources not held by individuals under a fee patent title belonged to all of the Navajo and that any revenue from any of this tribal land belonged to all of the people. To implement this Department of Interior policy, a "Business Council" was called in 1922, which Chee Dodge, Charley Mitchell, and Daagha'chii Bikiis attended at the invitation of the superintendents of the various Navajo jurisdictions concerned with oil and mineral leases. This business council was defined by Department of Interior officials as constituted to act in behalf of the Navajo Tribe, and it negotiated leases for reservation land for commercial purposes.

The Government administrators both on the local and departmental levels evidently had some misgivings about the nonelective status of the 1922 "Business Council" membership, for in the first month of 1923 the Commissioner of Indian Affairs, Charles H. Burke, issued a document entitled "Regulations Relating to the Navajo Tribe of Indians," which was approved on January 27 of that year by the Assistant Secretary of the Interior Department, F. M. Goodwin. These regulations made a point of stating that the Navajo were to be considered as a tribe-at-large in such matters as the administration of economic assets as oil, gas, coal, and other mineral deposits, tribal timber, and developments of underground water supply for stock purposes. The regulations also prescribed that there be appointed a Commissioner of the Navaho Tribe, who was to maintain a central office for management of the affairs of the entire tribe. The new commissioner was to have general supervision over each of the several superintendencies concerned with Navajo people.

The regulations also state that a Navajo Tribal Council was to be formed, and that this council was to work with the administrative officers of the Government on all matters concerning all of the Navajo. The Navajo Tribal Council was to be formed by the election of one delegate and one alternate delegate from each of the six superintendencies within Navajo country. Thus, the Tribal Council was to have representatives from the San Juan, Western Navajo, Southern Navajo, Pueblo Bonito, Leupp, the Moqui jurisdictions. The regulations did not specify how each delegate and alternate delegate was to be elected, but the responsibility for holding these elections was placed upon the superintendents of the six jurisdictions. In particular, the Indian Agents were to see that only "bona fide" Navajos living within each jurisdiction were elected to the Navajo Tribal Council. Thirty-days' election notice was to be given and, if the Navajos of a jurisdiction failed to elect a delegate and alternate delegate within that period, the Secretary of the Interior had the right to fill the positions with appointees.

The first order of business for the Tribal Council was to elect a chairman and vice-chairman. The Commissioner of the Navaho Tribe was to call for a meeting of the delegates and alternates and they as a group were to form a convention to elect the two officers of the Tribal Council. The chairman of the Tribal Council was to be selected from the Navajo Tribe-at-large and could not be either a delegate or an alternate to the Council. The Vice-Chairman, however, had to be selected from among the delegates. Both the delegates and alternates were allowed to cast one vote each for candidates for these offices, and the persons chosen by the members of the convention had to have a clear majority of the votes cast. The progress of the convention was to be guided by a temporary chairman who was selected under the "direction of the Commissioner to the Navaho Tribe" according to the set of rules and regulations adopted on January 27, 1923.

Once the chairman and vice-chairman had been elected, the convention was to dissolve and the Tribal Council was to convene. The role of the alternate delegate changed at this point: he was given the right to speak on issues during the council sessions, but he could vote only if the regular delegate was absent. The regular delegates were allowed to speak and cast one vote on issues before the council, and a majority of votes cast on an issue decided its fate. The vice-chairman had the right to speak and vote on any issue, but the chairman was allowed to speak on an issue only if he relinquished his position to the vice-chairman, and the chairman was allowed to vote only if a tie vote occurred. Records were to be kept of the proceedings of each council session and were to be forwarded to the Commissioner of Indian Affairs. The rules of January 27, 1923, stated that no meeting of the Navajo Tribal Council was to take place unless the Commissioner of the Navaho Tribe was present. In addition, the Secretary of the Interior reserved the right to remove any member of the Navajo Tribal Council, upon proper cause, and to require an election or appointment of some other delegate to take the place of the removed member.

321-627—70——3

It is evident that the Secretary of the Interior, as an agent for the Government of the United States, was willing to grant the Navajo only a limited measure of self-government. While the powers of the Council were not specifically circumscribed, it was to act as a forum to assist the Commissioner to the Navaho Tribe in managing the affairs of the Navajo people. The Secretary of the Interior held a heavy hand of influence over the Navajo Tribal Council, for he had the right to remove any council delegate and was able to determine when a council was to meet by acting through his subordinate, the Commissioner. In addition, the council was not allowed to conduct any meeting unless the Commissioner was present. Notwithstanding these limitations, the "Regulations Relating to the Navajo Tribe," stands as the first significant document leading to the development of greater self-government among the Navajo. In essence, it allowed Navajos to elect tribal leaders; leaders who were expected to express themselves on Government policies affecting the lives of the Navajo.

Earlier, we have noted that patterns among those Navajos practicing traditional culture included the selection of local leaders by elections, and that there was present the pattern of trying to reach a consensus of opinion. In view of these cultural patterns, the Government's plan of electing tribal leaders introducted two new political concepts. The first was that issues and elections were to be decided on the basis of a majority rule, and the second was the establishment of the political position within Navajo social organization of a popularly elected tribal-wide leader. In regard to the first innovation, we can only infer that the delegates and alternates were elected on a majority rule principle, as the procedure is not spelled out in the regulations. The regulations do, however, state that it was the responsibility of the superintendents of the various jurisdictions to see that elections were held and delegates and alternates were elected to fill these offices. Almost certainly, these superintendents (American Whites) employed the majority rule as a principle and a guide in these jurisdictional elections, even though it is possible to find Navajo informants at present (1962) who say that the delegates to the first councils were hand-picked by the various superintendents of the jurisdictions for their favorable attitude toward the Government. Nevertheless, once the delegates and alternates assembled they were required to proceed as a political body under the principle of majority rule.

The political structure proposed for the Navajo by the Government differs only slightly from that functioning in the United States generally at present. We note, by way of comparison, that the general public in the United States does not elect their president and vice-president directly, but elect a set of electors who in turn elect persons for these high political offices. The same pattern was suggested for Navajos, in that the delegates and alternates to the Tribal Council were to be elected by the general Navajo public, and these elected people in turn elected a chairman and vice-chairman. We can note an additional similarity in that the Electoral College of the United States disbands after performing its duty; the Navajo delegates and alternates cease to be an election convention once they have elected a chairman and vice-chairman to the Navajo Tribal Council. A difference in structure is found between the American political system and that which was proposed for the Navajo in that, among the latter, the convention representatives served in two different political positions and roles; that of convention delegate and of council delegate. In the American political system, the members of the Electoral College and members of Congress (which represent the American people on a geographical and numerical basis) are two different groups of people. In effect, the Navajo Tribal Council and the United States Congress are comparable political structures, but the Navajo Tribal Council was originally designed to elect the chiefs of state, whereas the primary function of the United States Congress is to legislate.[5] The outstanding functional difference between the Congress and the Council is that the latter was originally limited to advising and assisting the Commissioner to the Navaho Tribe in administering the needs of the Navajo people, with no powers of legislation; the primary function of the United States Congress is to pass laws that govern the American people. However, there is little doubt but that the model for the neophyte government for the Navajo was the political structure of the United States of America.

The first Navajo Tribal Council convened on July 7, 1923. Before this event occurred, however, a new set of rules and regulations concerning the formation of the Council was issued over the signatures of the Acting Commissioner of Indian Affairs, E. B. Meritt, and Secretary of the Interior Hubert Work (Young, 1961, p. 376). These new rules, dated April 24, 1923, superseded the January 27th document; thus the original set of rules was never used to organize a Navajo Tribal Council. The second set followed the general pattern of the first, but several minor and major changes were made in the later document.

The minor changes included a statement specifying that the Commissioner to the Navaho Tribe was the "agent in charge of the Navajo Reservation," whereas the earlier rules and regulations merely stated that he was to maintain a central office and have supervision over each of the superintendencies concerned with Navajo people. Another minor change was that interpreters were officially required for all Council meetings, so that English to Navajo and Navajo to English translations would insure a greater understanding by all participants. These translations would allow a recording clerk to make a more complete record of all that was said during a Council meeting, and these records were forwarded to the Commissioner of Indian Affairs in Washington, D.C., so that he would be able to keep abreast of Navajo attitudes and opinions. A third change of a minor nature was that the new rules reworded the phrase that the delegates and alternates "shall, under the direction of the Commissioner of the Navajo Tribe, appoint a temporary presiding officer" to conduct the proceedings to elect a chairman and vice-chairman of the Navajo Tribal Council to read, "the delegates to the convention shall appoint a temporary presiding officer from among their own number."

The two major changes increased the number of delegates from the more heavily populated jurisdictions and specified the number of years the chairman and vice-chairman were eligible to hold office.

The number of delegates to the Tribal Council was doubled to a total of 12 as follows: 3 from the San Juan jurisdiction (formerly 1); 2 from the Western Navajo jurisdiction (formerly 1); 4 from the Southern Navajo jurisdiction (formerly 1); 1 from the Pueblo Bonito jurisdiction (no change); 1 from the Leupp jurisdiction (no change); and 1 from the Moqui jurisdiction (no change). The number of alternate delegates was also increased in exactly the same proportion as the delegates. Thus, as both the delegates and alternates were allowed to vote in the convention, the body that selected the chairman and the vice-chairman of the Council totaled 24 under the new regulations. The new regulations retained the requirement that the chairman was to be selected from the tribe-at-large, and that the vice-chairman was to be selected from the group of delegates elected to the Council. The term of tenure for these offices was set at 4 years each, with the stipulation that no person could serve more than two terms in each office. Under the new rules, the Commissioner to the Navaho Tribe had the responsibility to call a convention when either the chairman's or vice-chairman's office was vacated by death, resignation, or at the end of a term.

A significant change in the role of the Secretary of the Interior in relation to the Navajo Tribal Council was incorporated through the deletion of the clause that had allowed him to remove any delegate "upon proper cause" and to provide for a new delegate to be either elected or

[5] The U.S. Congress is prescribed by law to elect a President and Vice-President only in the event that the Electoral College does not give any candidate a clear majority of its 537 votes. In 1824, the House of Representatives exercised its duty as prescribed by the 12th Amendment to the Constitution and elected John Quincy Adams over Andrew Jackson as President.

appointed to fill the vacant office. Thus, the potentially "heavy" hand of the Secretary was removed from the shoulders of the nascent Navajo Tribal Council.

The new rules made two additional changes governing the formation of the Council. The first was that only 10 days were allowed for Navajos to elect representatives to the Council, instead of the 30 days previously allowed. Second, the new regulations used and defined the word "quorum" in the text of the rules executed on April 24, 1923. A quorum was defined for the Navajo Tribal Council as two-thirds of the delegates, and the regulations stated that a quorum was a necessary condition for the transaction of Council business.

On July 7, 1923, the delegates and alternates gathered at Fort Defiance to hold a convention to elect a chairman and vice-chairman of the first Navajo Tribal Council. Chee Dodge was elected chairman by the delegates to the convention, but the position of vice-chairman was not filled (Young, 1961, p. 603). During the same day, the delegates under the guiding hand of Chee Dodge organized themselves into the first elected official body to sign oil and gas leases on behalf of the Navajo Tribe. Thus a limited self-government procedure was launched.

During the next 10 years the Council met for several days annually, and began to fulfill its role of advisor to the Commissioner to the Navaho Tribe. A few changes and amendments were made during this period: in 1927 the tenure both for delegates and officers of the Council was changed from 4-year to 5-year terms; in 1928, a third set of regulations (over the signature of Charles Burke, Commissioner of Indian Affairs) contained provisos that both men and women had the right to vote in all tribal elections, that the Commissioner of Indian Affairs was delegated the responsibility of calling the Navajo Tribal Council to session and that the term of office for *all* Council members (including chairman and vice-chairman) was 4 years.

The only other major change in the 1923 Council structure occurred in 1934, when the Navajo Tribal Council adopted a resolution amending the regulations to eliminate the position of alternate delegate and double the existing membership by declaring the alternates as full-fledged delegates to the Navajo Tribal Council. This action came as a result of Government pressure for the Navajo Tribal Council and the Navajo people-at-large to accept the provisions of the Indian Reorganization Act (Wheeler-Howard Act), which called for abandoning the existing Navajo Tribal Council and the formation of a government under a constitution (Young, 1961, p. 377). The Navajos voted by a slim margin of 7,992 to 7,608 to reject the Indian Reorganization Act. On November 24, 1936, however, the Navajo Tribal Council passed a resolution that established a committee to arrange a constitutional assembly for the purpose of writing and adopting a constitution for the Navajo (Council Resolutions, Nov. 24, 1936).

Under the direction of its chairman, Henry Tallman, and with the aid of Father Berard Haile, a Franciscan missionary to the Navajo (1900–1962), and Chee Dodge, the constitutional committee canvassed the reservation in order to identify the most influential headmen and explain to them the purpose of the proposed reorganization of the Council under a constitution. A total of 250 names of outstanding headmen was secured, from which a committee of 70 headmen was selected for membership in the proposed constitutional assembly. The constitutional committee was careful to choose headmen from all parts of the Navajo country, so that there would be full representation of all the people (Young, 1961, p. 379). The first meetings of the constitutional assembly were held on April 9 and 10, 1937, at which time the group voted 66–2 to declare itself to be, in fact, the Tribal Council and proceeded to draft a constitution and bylaws for the Navajo Tribe (Young, 1961, p. 380).

The second action of the constitutional assembly was to pass a resolution empowering the chairman of the assembly to appoint an executive committee to draw up a constitution. This resolution was passed 66–0 and Jacob Morgan, who led a small group of dissenters from the Council Hall immediately after denouncing the resolution, was appointed as the chairman of the constitutional committee. Within about 6 months this committee, composed of Jim Shirley as Chairman (Jacob Morgan having refused to serve), Robert Curley, Roy Hashkan, and Frank Miller with the assistance of Tom Dodge, sent to the Commissioner of Indian Affairs the proposed constitution for the Navajo. Thus, on October 25, 1937, the date the constitutional document was officially transmitted to the Bureau of Indian Affairs in Washington, D.C., the constitutional assembly had acomplished its purpose and was officially disbanded.

The proposed Navajo constitution was rejected by the Secretary of the Interior, "as it was generally agreed in view of the prevailing dissension and conflict [over a Government-sponsored livestock program] within the Tribe itself as well as between the Tribe and the Federal Government, that the time was not propitious for such a step" (Young, 1961, p. 381). Instead of the constitution, a set of bylaws was issued by the Secretary of the Interior, on July 26, 1938, which was sufficient only for the election and reorganization of a Navajo Tribal Council. The 1938 rules did not define the limits of authority of the new council and its officers, for it was hoped that the future Navajo electorate would agree to adopt a constitution by referendum. Since then, in effect, the Navajo have been represented on a tribal-wide basis by various councils elected under the 1938 "Rules for the Navajo

Tribal Council" as no constitution has been submitted to the Navajo for a vote.

Under the "new" rules of 1938 the membership of the Council was further enlarged to a total of 74 delegates with no alternates, and the Indian Commissioner no longer reserved the right to appoint delegates if the people failed to elect them or to fill vacancies on the Council. Equally important was the elimination of the requirement that all Council meetings had to be held in the presence of a Government official. The Commissioner of Indian Affairs, however, retained the right to call meetings, even though this was somewhat tempered in that he could exercise this right on the request of the Executive Committee of the Navajo Tribal Council.[6] The 1938 regulations specified the use of secret ballots and, for those who could not read, the identification of each candidate by a colored band. Majority rule governed which candidate was elected; in case a clear majority was not indicated among several candidates, a runoff election was called for.

The chairman and vice-chairman of the Navajo Tribal Council were not elected by the council membership under the 1938 Rules, but rather by popular vote of all Navajos over the age of 21 years. Candidates for the position of chairman were to be selected at provincial conventions. To accomplish this, Navajo country was divided into four provinces (map 6). Each election district from which a council delegate was chosen was to elect a representative to the nominating convention within the province. Each provincial convention chose, by majority vote, a single candidate for the position of chairman of the Navajo Tribal Council. The candidates from all four provincial conventions then were to be submitted to the Navajo in a general tribal-wide election. The successful candidate for chairman of the Navajo Tribal Council received a majority of the votes cast, and the candidate who received the next highest number of votes was elected to the office of vice-chairman. In the event that no candidate received a clear majority of the votes, runoff elections were required until one candidate obtained a clear majority.

The first election under the 1938 rules for Council delegates and its officers took place on September 24 of that year; Jacob Morgan was elected chairman and Howard Gorman was elected vice-chairman. The first meeting of the reorganized Council took place on November 8, 1938, and the Council has continued to operate under the 1938 rules to this date. Although, there have been no fundamental structural changes since 1938, there have been several modifications to those rules: pictorial ballots; allowance for off-reservation voting in such places as Los Angeles, Chicago, and Albuquerque; unlimited number of terms of office for the chairman and vice-chairman; and the acceptance of a write-in candidate for Council delegate. To date, a constitution for the Navajo has not been adopted, and the powers of the Council are nowhere defined or delimited, which means that the Navajo have never acted formally to recognize the Council as the governmental organization authorized to act on their behalf, and the Navajo Tribal Council is the creation of the Secretary of the Interior and subject to his will and direction or dissolution. It is important to point out, however, that the Navajo Tribal Council acts *as if* it had the authority to act on behalf of the Navajo.

The Navajo Tribal Council has gone through some modifications since it was formed in 1938, but it still remains an instrumentality of the Secretary of the Interior. In general, the Council has broadened its scope of action in recent years; a process of development excellently documented by Mary Shepardson (1963). However, the organizational structure of the Council remains the same as that developed under the 1938 rules, with the delegates to the Navajo Tribal Council being elected from 74 precincts both on and off the Navajo Reservation. There are 64 delegates elected from precincts that are inside the reservation boundary, and 10 elected from off-reservation areas.

The council delegates are elected every 4 years by popular vote, and each delegate must have obtained a majority of votes cast in his precinct. The Navajo Tribal Council meets regularly four times a year, usually in July, October, January, and May. Special sessions have been called occasionally in the past few years to deal with such problems as emergency stock feed programs. A majority of the Council must vote their approval for tribal activities that involve the spending of money derived from oil, coal, and gas leases, as well as approve multimillion-dollar budgets of various tribal offices and departments. Certain of the Council's authorities are delegated to an advisory committee comprised of Council delegates empowered to act for the Navajo Tribe during periods when the Council is not in session.[7]

At present a chairman and vice-chairman are elected to office every 4 years by popular vote. All the delegates of the Navajo Tribal Council are also elected anew each 4 years which means that there are no staggered terms of office for any elected tribal position, and therefore no necessary continuity of elected representatives from one administration to the next.

Since 1938, the Navajo Tribal Council has created a number of standing committees. These committees assist the Council by conducting studies and investigations in special areas, advise the Tribal Council of their findings, and suggest the initiation of certain programs by that

[6] The Executive Committee, designed to expedite routine business of the tribe when the Council is not in session, was to be composed of chief delegates chosen by fellow representatives from each of 19 land management districts (map 1).

[7] Established in 1947 by Council action; the nine members are chosen by the Chairman of the Navajo Tribal Council, who also decides when the advisory committee shall convene.

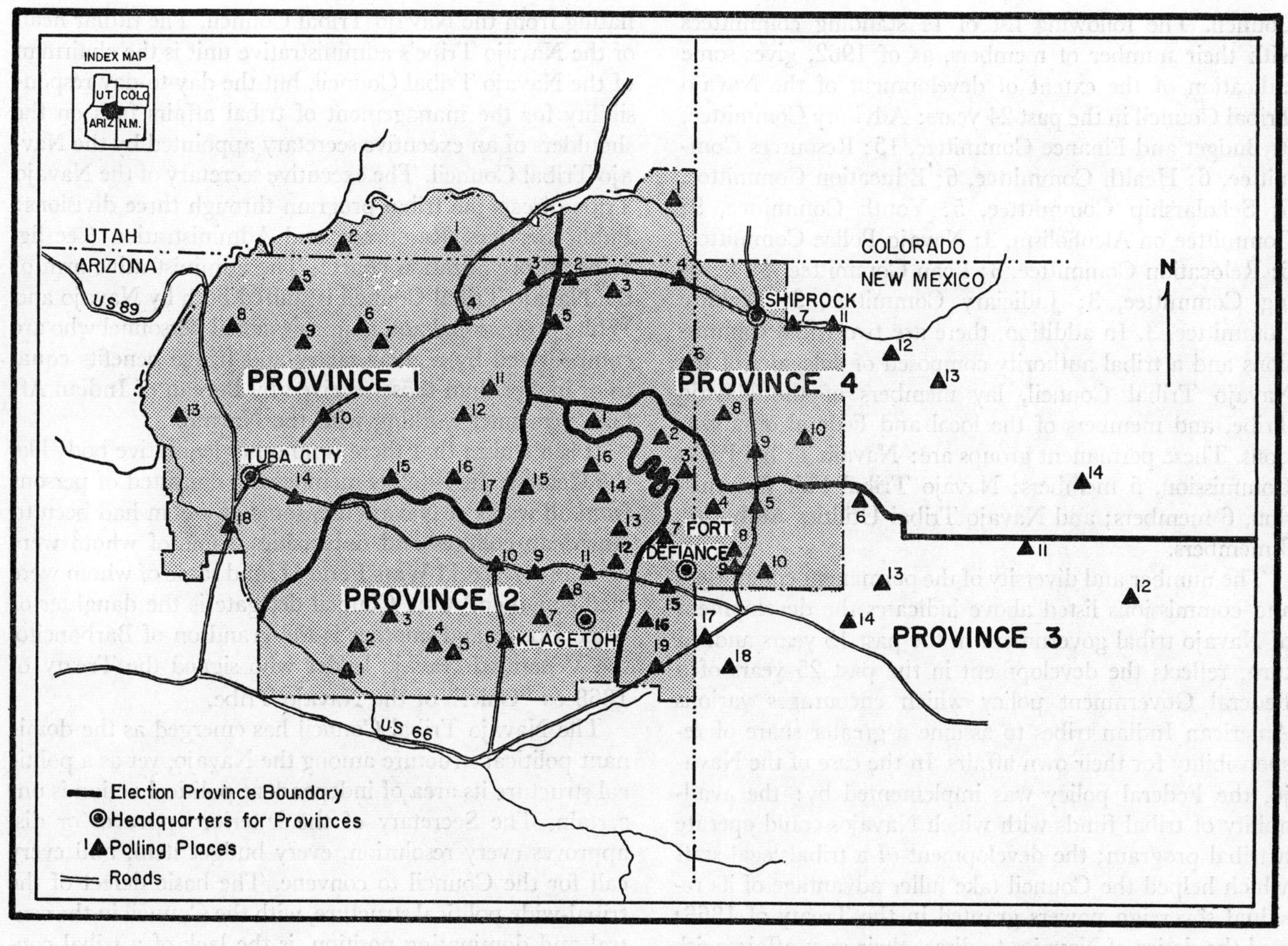

MAP 6.—Polling places in Navajo election provinces, 1960.

Province 1

1. Goulding Store
2. Navajo Mountain
3. Dennehotso
4. Kayenta
5. Lechee
6. Inscription House
7. Shonto
8. Copper Mine
9. Kaibito
10. Red Lake
11. Chilchinbito
12. Forest Lake
13. Bodaway
14. Coal Mine Mesa
15. Dinnebito Project
16. Piñon
17. Chinle Coalmine
18. Cameron

Province 2

1. Leupp
2. Tolani Springs
3. Bird Spring
4. Cedar Springs
5. Dilcon
6. Indian Wells
7. Greasewood
8. Cornfields
9. Steamboat
10. Jeddito
11. Ganado
12. Kin Li Chee
13. Nazlini
14. Chinle
15. Black Mountain
16. Many Farms

Province 3

1. Round Rock
2. Lukachukai
3. Tsailee
4. Crystal
5. Naschitti
6. Lake Valley
7. Sawmill
8. Tohatchi
9. Mexican Springs
10. Coyote Canyon
11. Pueblo Pintado
12. Torreon
13. Crownpoint
14. Mariana Lake
15. St. Michaels
16. Oak Springs
17. Manuelito
18. Two Wells
19. Houck

Province 4

1. Aneth
2. Mexican Water
3. Sweet Water
4. Teec Nos Pos
5. Rock Point
6. Red Rock
7. Fruitland
8. Sanasti
9. Nava
10. Burnham
11. Nenahnezad
12. Bloomfield Store
13. Huerfano
14. Nageezi

Council. The following list of 14 standing committees with their number of members, as of 1962, gives some indication of the extent of development of the Navajo Tribal Council in the past 24 years: Advisory Committee, 9; Budget and Finance Committee, 15; Resources Committee, 6; Health Committee, 6; Education Committee, 6; Scholarship Committtee, 5; Youth Committee, 9; Committee on Alcoholism, 3; Navajo Police Committee, 6; Relocation Committee, 3; Loan Committee, 4; Trading Committee, 3; Judiciary Committee, 3; Welfare Committee, 3. In addition, there are two tribal commissions and a tribal authority composed of delegates of the Navajo Tribal Council, lay members of the Navajo Tribe, and members of the local and Federal organizations. These permanent groups are: Navajo Tribal Parks Commission, 5 members; Navajo Tribal Fair Commission, 6 members; and Navajo Tribal Utilities Authority, 3 members.

The number and diversity of the permanent committees and commissions listed above indicates the development of Navajo tribal government in the past 15 years and, in turn, reflects the development in the past 25 years of a Federal Government policy which encourages various American Indian tribes to assume a greater share of responsibility for their own affairs. In the case of the Navajo, the Federal policy was implemented by: the availability of tribal funds with which Navajos could operate a tribal program; the development of a tribal legal staff which helped the Council take fuller advantage of its residual sovereign powers granted in the Treaty of 1868; and the desire of Navajos to direct their own affairs with a minimum of interference from Federal and State governments (Young, 1961, p. 390).

A concomitant development to the above was the formation of a bureaucracy to administer the directives emanating from the Navajo Tribal Council. The titular head of the Navajo Tribe's administrative unit is the chairman of the Navajo Tribal Council, but the day-to-day responsibility for the management of tribal affairs falls on the shoulders of an executive secretary appointed by the Navajo Tribal Council. The executive secretary of the Navajo Tribe directs the tribal program through three divisions: Public Services, Resources, and Administration (see fig. 1 for an organization chart). The administrative arm of the Navajo Tribal Council is staffed both by Navajo and White professional and nonprofessional personnel who are compensated by regular salary and fringe benefits equal to or higher than those received by Bureau of Indian Affairs personnel working with the Navajo.

It is a truism that there is no other legislative body like the Council. In 1962 its membership consisted of persons from all walks of Navajo life, some of whom had been to American colleges and universities, some of whom were veterans of World Wars I and II, and some of whom were medicine men.[8] One Council delegate is the daughter of Chee Dodge and another is the grandson of Barboncito, the Venerated Navajo leader who signed the Treaty of 1868 as "Chief" of the Navajo Tribe.

The Navajo Tribal Council has emerged as the dominant political structure among the Navajo, yet as a political structure its area of independent political action is uncertain. The Secretary of the Interior approves or disapproves every resolution, every budget item, and every call for the Council to convene. The basic defect of the tribal-wide political structure, with the Council in the central and dominating position, is the lack of a tribal constitution. Thus the Council remains structurally and functionally dependent upon and responsive to an agency of the Government, the Department of Interior, and not to the Navajo people, who elect its members.

GRAZING COMMITTEES

There were two major areas of activity of the Navajo Tribal Council during the first years of its existence. The first was the negotiation and signing of land leases for the exploitation of sections of the Navajo Reservation by commercial corporations seeking deposits of oil and other minerals. This task was handled relatively efficiently by the Council, inasmuch as they delegated responsibility to the Commissioner to the Navaho Tribe, a person appointed by the Commissioner of Indian Affairs. The second major area of activity concerned the multifaceted problem of an expanding Navajo population dependent almost exclusively on livestock, yet occupying an area of insufficient grazing resources.

This concern led to the creation of a new sociopolitical structure, the District Grazing Committee, through the joint effort of the Navajo Tribal Council and the Government. The history of this development indicates the difficulties encountered in a program of directed culture change.[9] The Government, through several of its agencies, embarked upon a program of voluntary stock reduction

[8] Two very reliable Navajo informants gave as 39 the number of medicine men in the 1962 Navajo Tribal Council. In addition both the chairman and vice-chairman were medicine men and could perform Sings.

[9] Among Navajos, quantity rather than quality is most frequently accorded greater value. Thus, the more sheep and goats a Navajo owns, the higher his status. Of equal importance is the Navajo cultural theme that each living thing has a right to live and reach its potential.

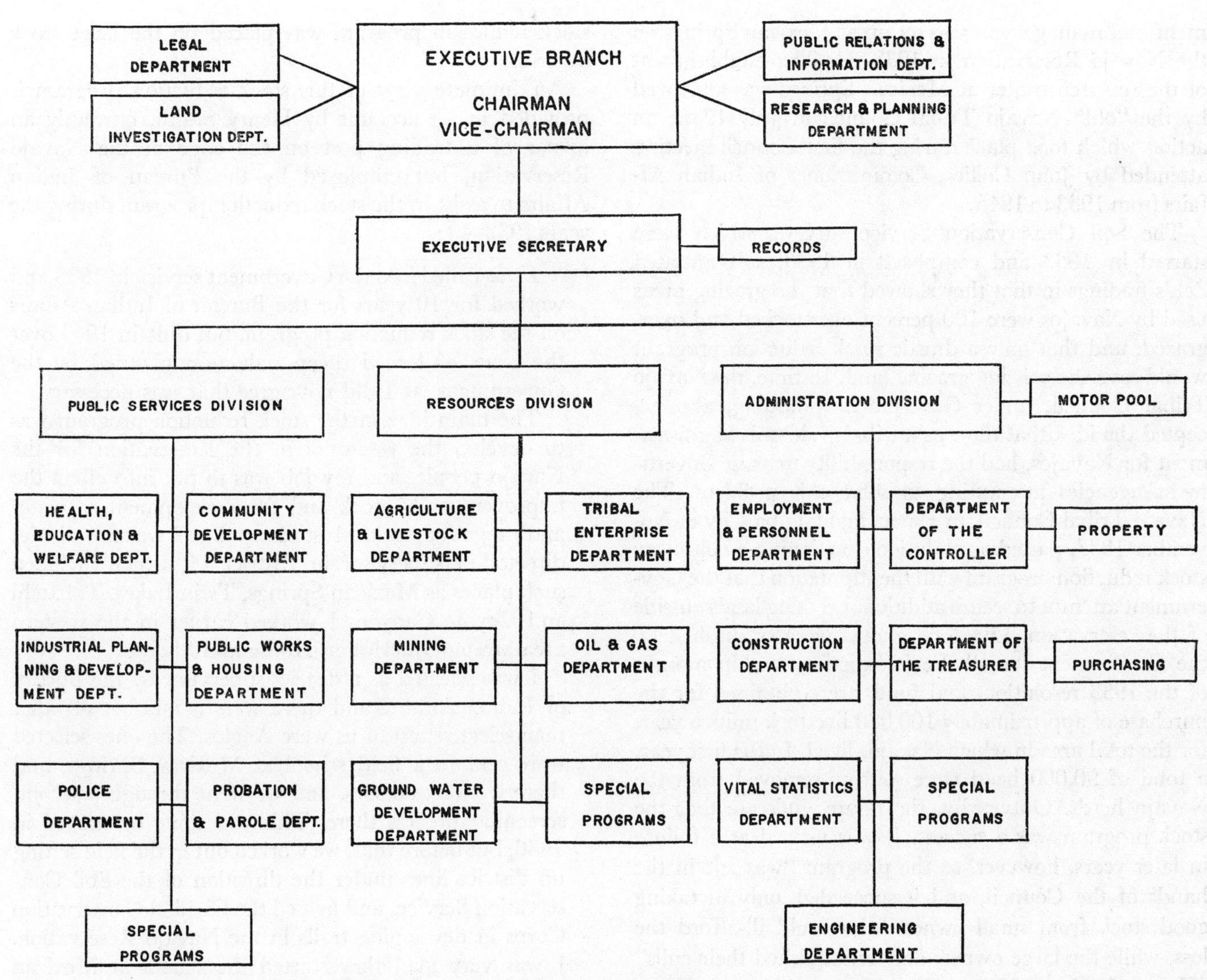

FIGURE 1.—Organization of the executive branch of the Navajo Tribe, 1959. Adopted by Resolution No. 50–59 of the Navajo Triba Council on August 6, 1959.

and improvement in the 1930's, but later switched to a forced program when the people balked and ceased to cooperate. The Government's stock reduction program among the Navajo was no less than a major social and economic revolution which continues to the present day (Young, 1961, p. 151).

The Navajo population had grown from between 9,000–10,000 in 1868 to about 15,500 in 1880, then up to 22,455 in 1910, and it had reached nearly 40,000 by 1930 (Young, 1961, p. 147). The Government, primarily through the office of the President, had increased the size of the Navajo Reservation from 3,500,000 acres in 1868, to nearly 12,000,000 acres in 1930 (see map 3, p. 13). As the population grew, the number of sheep, goats, cattle and horses also increased; from about 45,000 units in 1868, to over 1,000,000 units in 1930. The increased number of livestock units, which is determined by how much forage one mature sheep consumes in a year, severely taxed the grazing areas in the Navajo country which had been plagued with droughts of several years' duration from time to time. In 1930, William H. Zeh, an Indian Bureau Forester, submitted a report documenting the fact that the grazing resources of the Navajo were being rapidly depleted and eroded away, especially around the major watering holes. It was Zeh's opinion that the primary cause of the erosion of the reservation's grazing resources was the overstocking of the ranges. He suggested that a soil conservation program be instituted to include stock reduction, stock improvement, and an educational program designed to show both the younger and older stockmen proper methods of range management and livestock improvement (Young, 1961, p. 150). In line with Zeh's recommendations, the Soil Conservation Service conducted a number of surveys in Navajo country to determine the extent of erosion and overstocking of Navajo ranges. A research center for range improvement and management was set up at Mexican Springs on the Navajo Reservation in 1933–34. The establishment of the research center at Mexican Springs was approved by the "old" Navajo Tribal Council in July 1933; an action which took place during the first Council meeting attended by John Collier, Commissioner of Indian Affairs from 1933 to 1945.

The Soil Conservation Service surveys, which were started in 1933 and completed in 1935, substantiated Zeh's findings in that they showed that the grazing areas used by Navajos were 100 percent overstocked and overgrazed, and that only a drastic stock reduction program would save the existing grazing land. In time, the Navajo Tribal Council, under Government prodding, also accepted the idea that they, as a tribal-wide unit of government for Navajos, had the responsibility to assist Government agencies attempting to solve this problem. The Navajo Tribal Council, in a meeting at Tuba City in November 1933, passed a resolution sanctioning a voluntary stock reduction program with the stipulation that the Government attempt to secure additional grazing lands outside of the reservation. Livestock quotas were established by the Government for all the jurisdictions within months of the 1933 resolution, and funds were obtained for the purchase of approximately 100,000 livestock units a year, for the total area in which Navajos lived. In the first year, a total of 90,000 head were sold or removed from the Navajo herds. Outwardly, the figures indicate that the stock program was a success. It was viewed as a failure in later years, however, as the program "was left in the hands of the Council, and it succeeded only in taking good stock from small owners who could ill-afford the loss, while the large owners only relinquished their culls" (Young, 1961, p. 153).

The stock reduction program touched nearly every Navajo family in Navajo country, and when the Government urged the Council at a 1934 meeting at Fort Defiance to adopt a resolution that further stock reductions were necessary, the Council refused to comply.

Very likely the members of the Navajo Tribal Council were reflecting the attitudes of most Navajos, who viewed the stock reduction program with "alarm and suspicion, seeing in its operation a threat to their survival" (Young 1961, p. 153). It was difficult for the majority of the Navajo to equate money or wages with the traditional measure of wealth—namely, livestock—even though the outstanding leader of this period, Chee Dodge, had repeatedly advised them to adopt other forms of wealth (Underhill, 1956, p. 232). Compromises were eventually worked out so that between 1930 and 1935 the sheep and goat population was reduced from about 1,300,000 to 950,000 (Young, 1961, p. 154). By 1934 a general policy began to take shape in which the brunt of the stock reduction program was placed on the large stock owners.

An intimate view of this stock reduction program is provided in an account by Henry Smith, currently an owner of a trading post on the edge of the Navajo Reservation, but employed by the Bureau of Indian Affairs to assist in the stock reduction program during the years 1933–43:

> I was called into the Government service in 1933 and worked for 10 years for the Bureau of Indian Affairs on the stock reduction program, but quit in 1943 over the issue of forced sheep reduction planned by the Government, as I did not agree that was necessary.
>
> The main idea of the stock reduction program was to develop the resources in the Reservation for the Navajo people, and my job was to put into effect the improvement of stock and the development of water and range for stock. Most of my time I was the district director or supervisor in District 14, which included such places as Mexican Springs, Twin Lakes, Tohatchi and Coyote Canyon. I worked earlier in the western area around Inscription House and Shonto.
>
> I was selected as a district supervisor by the Bureau of Indian Affairs, and there were a number of other men selected; all of us were Anglos. The ones selected were sent to a field school at Mexican Springs, and there we took courses, and we went through a second screening process there. This was done or started in 1936, but before that, we worked out in the field setting up district lines under the direction of the Soil Conservation Service, and helped the Civilian Conservation Corps in developing trails in the Navajo Reservation. I was very glad they started the school at Mexican Springs, for there is a need of a buffer between the U.S. Government specialist such as the soil conservationist and the Navajo people, and the "school" taught us how to act as a buffer. Van Valkenburgh was probably the most important idea-man at the Mexican Springs research center, and he should be given most of the credit for the program. [Interview; April 5, 1962.]

The informant told how he was able to get Navajos to give or sell stock on a voluntary basis by getting the big stock owners to agree to the program; the smaller owners would then follow their lead. His technique was to convince the big owners that they should get rid of the poorly developed sheep, goats, and horses.

> The large stock owners among the Navajos were the leaders in their areas. . . . One such man in the Kaibito area was regarded very highly because he controlled antelope, and all other Navajos around there left antelope alone, and once I got him convinced to

go along on the voluntary program everyone else did too. [Ibid.]

However, the leaders in the eastern area of the reservation around Twin Lakes originally disagreed with the stock program, and would not cooperate. Smith recalled that, in 1947, when horses were forcibly reduced

Jake Morgan strongly objected to the program, and he took all of the horses to a location off of the reservation, so we could not get them. But we got them anyway by telling the people we had their horses and we would take them all unless they came down and identified their horses, and select the ones they were allowed to keep, as we were willing to let them keep the best horses. The very next day the Navajos came down and identified their horses and saved the best of their stock. Also, at times some Navajo men would follow me around and when quotas had been agreed upon, they would tell the people to forget all that I had told them, and hide their sheep. However, I guess I had much less trouble than most of the district supervisors, for I spoke Navajo fairly well, and we got along with each other. In my district [14] we got our quotas and it was handled fair and square. The quotas were set up in 1936, and this was done on the basis of dipping records and census data. However, when the Government insisted on forced reduction of sheep and goats in 1942, and this caused widespread resentment, I resigned in protest, for it caused more harm than good.

[In response to questions concerning the formation of the various district grazing areas or land management districts, he said:]

There were two criteria used. The first and really the most important was community interest, and this was based upon an area of land traditionally used by certain families or, in other words, a land-use community; the land the people in the community had, the land they used to herd their sheep and goats. The ultimate size of the land management district was determined by the general requirements of service by the BIA and management of the area by personnel.

The second criterion used was "natural areas" or the limiting features of the natural landscape. We used the ridges of the mountains in areas, the edges of canyons, the boundaries of the Navajo Reservation, and the edges of the arid sections to determine the district lines.

Grazing districts were set up by the Soil Conservation Service so that each area encompassed approximately 1,000,000 acres, and each general grazing district was subdivided into smaller sections or precincts on the basis of 500 Navajos per unit. A rangerider was assigned to each of these precincts, and it was his responsibility to carry out the directives of the district supervisor, who was in turn responsible to the Commissioner to the Navaho Tribe. Eventually, there were organized 19 land management districts or grazing districts which included both reservation and non-reservation areas.[10] The subunits of the grazing districts were utilized as election precincts when the Navajo Tribal Council was reorganized in 1936, thereby theoretically providing, one Council delegate for every 500 Navajos. These election precincts have remained essentially the same to the present time, and have not been altered to provide for a more equitable per capita representation of the greatly increased Navajo population.

Currently, the grazing districts or land management districts and their subdivisions are the basic political units among the Navajo population living in the three States of Arizona, New Mexico, and Utah. The Government, acting in accordance with its general policy of promoting self-government among the various Indian Tribes in the United States, strongly urged the Navajo Tribal Council to officially support the stock reduction program. Thus, on November 12, 1936, the Council passed a resolution setting up a special committee which had the responsibility for formulating a set of regulations governing grazing of stock on the reservation. The special committee reported to the Council on June 2, 1937, and presented a code or set of rules and regulations for the grazing of livestock on the Navajo Reservation. This code was approved by the membership of the 1936 Council, and the Government's voluntary stock reduction and range improvement had the official blessing of the Navajo tribal government. The management of the program remained in the hands of the Bureau of Indian Affairs, however, as it continued to appoint and supervise the grazing district directors and the rangeriders.

A virtual storm of protest broke over the heads of the Navajo councilmen who participated in the resolution supporting the stock reduction program, and many Navajos found it hard to believe that "our leaders agreed to sell what we live by" (Underhill, 1956, p. 238). The delegates excused themselves by saying that they had no choice in the matter. This, however, did not satisfy the Navajo people for they saw the Government agents hauling off their sheep, goats, and horses to be slaughtered or sold in violation of their traditional pattern of belief that everything has a right to live out its natural life. In addition, sheep, goats, and horses were traditionally a measure of well-being and wealth among Navajos, and the American money they received was not of equal value.

The intensity of the emotions aroused in Navajos as a result of the Council approving the stock reduction pro-

[10] Grazing District No. 6 encompasses an area used almost exclusively by Hopi Indians.

321-627—70——4

gram can be measured by the fact that Navajos in 1962 still remember those men in their localities who voted to approve the resolution, and the indications are that these men today are considered politically untrustworthy. In a 1960 political gathering in the southwestern section of the reservation, a Navajo who had voted for the stock reduction code in 1936 was described as

> ". . . a man who voted against his people, and now he is here asking us older people to tell him about how we lived before and after *Huelte* [Fort Sumner period of 1864–68]. I am asking myself if we can trust him with this information."

There is also a statement by the chairman of the Navajo Tribal Council on September 25, 1961, in which he said:

> There has been a feeling on my part that I was not a party to accepting the grazing regulations as accepted by the Tribe. I have insisted on standing on the humanitarian standpoint rather than adhering to the law as accepted by the Tribe. That is to say that where we have no job and a few sheep to depend on, I would not permit those sheep to be released because they happen to be two, three, or four over the permitted number. People are solely dependent on a subsistence living, and it was thought by me that I would be that hard on my people and I won't unless conditions improve. I would not adhere to the full impact of carrying out the grazing regulations.
>
> I can't help repeating that those people who are in worse condition—and I will have to admit that it was pitiful and I can't say to myself that regardless of how you are, I am going to have to enforce regulations. From the beginning, I have stood on that platform and I will stand on it to the point when conditions improve, when conditions warrant that we follow the grazing regulations of our country. If not, they would have to throw me out of office first before I would carry out the full regulation of our land as far as grazing is concerned. [Navajo Reservation Central Grazing Committee, 1961, p. 2.]

Navajos in general still oppose limiting the number of livestock a family may own, but the high point of resistance to the program occurred in 1943 when sheep and goats were forcibly reduced. Opposition has gradually diminished since that time, primarily due to economic changes brought about by the large number of Navajos working for wages away from home. By 1952, the Navajo Tribal Council was willing to vote approval of a resolution (CA–30–52) requesting that the Secretary of the Interior authorize the establishment of tribal grazing committees in each grazing district. This request was approved by the Secretary of the Interior on October 28, 1952, and the council set in motion a series of actions which resulted in the formation of district grazing committees in all land management districts within the reservation, and the creation of a number of district land boards to function as grazing committees for those Navajos living in off-reservation areas.

The Council's first move was to pass Resolution CJ–6–53 on January 13, 1953, which recommended that the advisory committee initiate the establishment of grazing committees in all of the districts within the reservation boundaries. The advisory committee acted upon the request on February 20, 1953, and by Resolution ACF–14–53 adopted a handbook entitled "Navajo Reservation Grazing Committees, Their Duties and Responsibilities." In succeeding years—once in 1957 and again in 1962—the handbook was modified in minor ways, but the general grazing committee structure has remained the same since its adoption in 1953.

The central and controlling position in the grazing committee structure is occupied by the advisory committee, which calls itself the Central Grazing Committee when it deals with matters of grazing regulations. The Tribal Resources Committee of the Navajo Tribal Council acts as a subordinate body to the Central Grazing Committee, but the resources committee members do not have the privilege of voting on issues brought before the Central Grazing Committee. The Navajo Tribal Council can pass resolutions affecting grazing operations among Navajos living on the reservation, as can the advisory committee. Thus, the central grazing committee acts as a link between these two political bodies and the district grazing committees. The Secretary of the Interior, however, has the final decision over all resolutions from either the advisory committee or the Council, and ultimate control is still in the hands of the Government.

The handbook on grazing regulations specifies that each land management district shall have one grazing committee composed of as many members as there are delegates to the Navajo Tribal Council from that district, with the exception of district 15 which includes land both within and outside the reservation. The land within the reservation in district 15 elects one delegate to the Council. For the administration of grazing regulations, however, the delegate precinct was divided into three parts, each of which elects a committeeman to the grazing committee for district 15. Thus the number of Council delegates elected from areas or precincts within the Navajo Reservation totals 64, but there are 66 grazing committee members because the district 15 on-reservation precinct elects two additional committee members.

It is the responsibility of each Navajo Tribal Council delegate, following his election, to call a meeting of the people of his precinct for the purpose of electing a person to serve as a representative to the district grazing committee. The committeeman is elected by a majority of people present at the meeting, and the results are transmitted to the chairman of the Navajo Tribal Council. The election of a grazing committee representative is to be held by July 1st of the year in which a general election of delegates and officers to the Navajo Tribal Council is held. Council delegates are eligible for the office of committeeman, unless they are members of the Advisory or Tribal Resources Committees, and often run for the position. The term of office is approximately 4 years, as each incumbent serves through June 30th of an election year.

Each district grazing committee is required to hold one meeting a month and may hold as many as 120 a year, for which each member is paid a per diem allowance of $18 plus 10 cents a mile for travel to and from the meeting. District grazing committees are instructed to elect one of their members to be chairman, one to be vice-chairman, and one person to serve as secretary. The regulations suggest that at least one district grazing committee member be able to speak, read, and write English. In the event that a district grazing committee elect a Council delegate to the office of chairman, the vice-chairman is required to be a non-Council delegate so that the business of the committee can be carried on when the Navajo Tribal Council is in session.

The duties and responsibilities of the district grazing committees include organizing and conducting the sheep and goat dipping, spraying, or dusting program; branding activities; livestock disease prevention programs; surplus livestock removal programs; and assisting the Superintendent of the Navajo Agency and his authorized representatives in obtaining the annual livestock count. The grazing committee members are to hold scheduled meetings to explain the grazing regulations to stockmen, and to cooperate with the tribe and the Bureau of Indian Affairs with conservation programs and all matters pertaining to obtaining or disposing of grazing permits for stockmen. The district grazing committee is asked to serve as mediator in adjusting and settling range disputes between stockmen within their respective districts, and they are advised to help the parties in dispute to seek a mutual settlement of difficulties and not to assume the role of judge and jury.

In addition to the duties and responsibilities connected with livestock, the district grazing committee assigns land-use permits in small irrigation projects involving small-acreage farms and approves or disapproves the use of land for residences in communities such as Fort Defiance. In general, the district grazing committees determine the use of land that lies within each district, and policy is activated by the use of parliamentary procedures such as quorum and majority rules.

A completely separate political organization has been created to serve those Navajos living off (but within about 100 miles) of the reservation who are engaged in livestock raising and other subsistence techniques that involve the use of land. There are three land management districts that lie outside of the Navajo Reservation and in which there are organized land boards that perform essentially the same function as do the on-reservation district grazing committees. These district land boards were authorized under the Resolution of the Advisory Committee No. ACO–38–54, passed by them on October 19, 1954. This resolution states that there shall be one district land board for district 15 (off)[11], 16, and 19, and that each district land board shall consist of three members, except in the areas where the volume of work justifies additional members. The same resolution states that the advisory committee of the Navajo Tribal Council is to be the central land board which can approve a request that a district land board membership be increased up to a total of five members.

The land board members are elected, at an annual meeting on or before June 15th, by the land users in a district. The term of office for each member is set at 3 years, but the first (1954) land boards were elected to serve staggered terms of office; one-, two-, and three-years, respectively. Thus, they normally have a continuity of experienced members. The land boards are formally organized like the district grazing committees, in that each elects a chairman, vice-chairman, and a secretary, and no person serving on the advisory committee can be a member of a district land board.

The members of the land boards receive the same per diem and travel allowances as do the district grazing committeemen, but instead of 120 days of allowable meetings (for which members are paid) the land board members can hold up to 160 meetings a year. The increase is correlated with an enlarged function of the land boards for, in addition to the duties and responsibilities of a grazing and land-use nature, land board members are expected to cooperate and work with the U.S. Forest Service, State land boards, and the Bureau of Land Management on mutual problems, especially in the issuing of land-use permits in Government owned forests and ranges.

The Navajos in off-reservation areas have a second kind of grazing organization that operates informally insofar as the Navajo Tribe is concerned but that is recognized by the Bureau of Land Management of the Navajo Agency, Bureau of Indian Affairs. These unofficial grazing committees are found in 34 "communities" in off-reservation areas, and usually they elect a chairman, vice-chairman, and a secretary. While they do not receive any pay for their service, they advise and assist the district land boards in their duties and operations.

There are land boards for the major irrigation projects

[11] Grazing District 15 includes land areas within and outside of the Navajo Reservation; thus "District 15 (off)" is used by the U.S. Government and the Navajo Tribe officials to designate the area outside of the Navajo Reservation proper.

at Many Farms, Hogback, Fruitland, Ganado, Red Lake, and Moencopi-Tuba City which were authorized as a tribal organization by the Advisory Committee Resolution ACO–38–54, passed on October 19, 1954. These land boards were organized along lines identical to those of the off-reservation land boards and operate in a similar fashion, with the exception that the on-reservation land boards are concerned solely with permits for land use in the areas of these large irrigation projects. Membership on a major irrigation land board is restricted to those Navajos living in the area of the project.

Over a period of about 20 years, the Navajo have made an adjustment in their way of life concerning controlled grazing of livestock and land use. Nevertheless there were noncompliance statements from the chairman of the Navajo Tribal Council in 1961, indicating that restrictions were not fully accepted. A number of important factors contributed to this shift of opinion and action regarding limitation and restricted use of land: long periods of drought; participation in the Armed Forces during World War II and the Korean War; employment during World War II in war-related industries; on- and off-reservation wagework; and the general decline of the sheep market. Also, during the same 25-year period the Navajo population more than doubled itself: a pastoral economy that was failing to support a population of about 30,000 people in 1930, certainly was not able to support nearly double that number in 1950 (Young, 1961, p. 162). Younger Navajo men and women who returned, from wage earning jobs and educational institutions, to the reservation and to their family's hogan were often unwilling to return to the traditional Navajo ways of making a living. Some of these younger Navajos sought part-time or semiannual wage paying jobs off the reservation doing such work as harvesting crops, working on railroads, fruit picking, construction work, and broom making, while others took office jobs with the Bureau of Indian Affairs or in one of the Navajo Tribe's emerging governmental agencies. Still others used their G.I. Bill of Rights benefits to obtain additional education or a loan for a small business. Only a few young Navajos returned to the ways of their grandfathers and herded sheep as a means of making a living.

The older people of the Navajo Tribe had little choice but to try to salvage what they could from an outmoded subsistence pattern, and it is to their credit that they have succeeded so well in the face of harsh winters and a steady decline in range forage. However, these traditionally oriented Navajos have not been left to the mercy of nature, for a water development program involving nearly $7,000,000 (jointly financed by the Navajo Tribe and the Government) was put into operation during 1950–60. In addition, an emergency feed program was initiated in 1957 and repeated in 1958 and 1959, in which over 151 million pounds of grain—at a cost of nearly $6,000,000—were provided for Navajo livestock owners. However, these pump-priming activities can be considered only a rearguard action on the part of the Navajo tribal government and the Government, for the degree and extent to which the Navajo depend upon livestock has declined drastically during the past 20 years (Young, 1961, p. 164). It is reported that as recently as 1940, 58.4 percent of all reservation income was derived from stock raising and agriculture, whereas in 1960 these two activities accounted for only 10 percent of the total reservation income (Young, 1961, p. 164).

In general, the men and women elected to serve as members of either the land boards or the district grazing committees are oriented toward maintaining a traditional Navajo way of life aimed at retaining stock raising as the basis of their economy. These Navajos are generally middle-aged, are livestock owners themselves, and, in some cases, are the same people who resisted the Government stock reduction program in 1930–40. I surmise, that these older Navajos maintain their respect and position as leaders in their "communities" by opposing the stock reduction program, and were elected to serve on grazing committees because the general Navajo electorate felt that these elder traditionally oriented Navajos might be able to stem the tide of stock reduction if they were in a controlling position. This conjecture is given support by the July 1962 statement of a district grazing committeeman from the Houck area, who said:

> We must not knuckle-down and accept the ruling by the U.S. Government on enforced stock reduction, down to the limit permitted us by the Bureau, just to get some extra feed. I say, let us wait and see what develops. We have had enough of orders from Washington, and it is time we started looking to our grandfather's way, and send our thoughts to them. Anytime Washington gives something away, they get a lot more back, so I say, follow the good way, our way!

This statement came in response to the announcement from the Bureau of Indian Affairs that the Commissioner would approve expenditures of money for emergency livestock purchase or emergency feed only if the livestock permit holders reduced their stock to the allowable number, and only if those Navajos without permits to graze stock got rid of their sheep and goats.

It seems as though the hope is still alive that the Navajo can return to a pastoral way of life, and by doing so retain their traditional cultural patterns and values. This expression of hope is channeled into votes for those members of their "communities" to represent them in the district grazing committees and district land boards. It is to be noted that all Navajos in an election precinct can vote for candidates to these offices, and that voting is not restricted to those people who hold grazing permits. The traditional Navajo cultural orientation that most of these committee members hold in regard to Governmental control has not prevented them from assuming active roles in the Government and Council sponsored livestock administrative units. The most probable reasons behind this participation are that it provides an income of $2,000 to $3,000 a year; an official position from which one can object to the stock reduction program; and a base of operations and a small degree of authority to develop good livestock and range management habits among fellow Navajos. The acceptability of the new sociopolitical structure in the form of grazing committees and land boards among contemporary Navajos is understandable only if we take into consideration the fact that most of the people elected to positions within this new structure are at odds with its basic tenet or purpose—that of controlling the number of sheep, goats, and horses a Navajo man may own. The men and women elected to fill grazing committee positions, judging by observable criteria, are oriented toward a traditional Navajo way of life.[12] These individuals live in scattered hogan-camp settlements, speak little or no English, are active in traditional curing ceremonies either as Singers or as guest speakers, are wary and shy of strangers, and engage in pastoralism as their major subsistence pattern to support members of their extended family with whom they live.

Most grazing committee members interviewed by me represented themselves as being opposed to Governmental or tribal interference in livestock matters, and in public speeches stated they were in opposition to controlled livestock management by any institutionalized agency. However, most grazing committee members actively participated in such Government-sponsored programs as sheep dipping and vaccination of herds to prevent stock losses due to disease. In addition, almost all grazing committee members were extremely active in recent tribal programs of emergency feed and grain distribution to Navajo stockmen during harsh winters. Thus, on close examination it is found that the opposition Navajos have to Governmental interference is not consistent and complete. The opposition is centered almost exclusively on the restrictions imposed by the new structure on the number of livestock units an individual may own and where an individual may graze his stock.

In substance, grazing committee members support any Governmental or tribal program that aids them in maintaining and increasing individual holdings of sheep, goats, and horses, yet at the same time members are equally active and vocal in demanding that all restrictions be removed on the number of sheep units an individual may own. It is therefore inferred that these grazing committee members are attempting to reestablish the traditional pattern of pastoralism as a way of life for the Navajo people, and by doing so have placed themselves in direct opposition to the Government's program of directed culture change.

EARLY NAVAJO CHAPTERS

The third major political institution among contemporary Navajos is the local organization known by them as the "chapter." The idea of organizing Navajos into chapters—as with the Navajo Tribal Council and the district grazing committees—was introduced to the Navajo by agents of the Government. In contrast to the latter two political units, which were the product of ideas formulated on the departmental level in Washington, D.C., chapters were conceptualized and put into form on the local agency administrative level.

The person responsible for the introduction of chapters among the Navajo was John G. Hunter (pl. 1), Superintendent of the Leupp Agency located in the southwestern section of Navajo country. It was noted earlier (p. 1) that Hunter reported the need to "reach" more Navajos in order to administer to their needs. He first thought of annually having one or more general meetings of all Navajos within agency jurisdiction, but after the first general meeting in 1927, he decided that the large number of people who attended made such a meeting unmanageable. His solution was to divide the Leupp Agency into five sections, and have the Navajos in each section hold "community councils" four or five times a year. The yearly meeting was retained, but the "chiefs" of these five community councils were held responsible for bringing issues to the notice of the agency personnel.

The success of Hunter's experiment has overshadowed several other local governmental developments that took place at about the same time. Two of these are described below to indicate that, in several areas at least, Navajos were being introduced to procedures such as election by simple majority and the recording of minutes of a meeting. The first incident is probably one of the earliest attempts

[12] An apparent exception is this grazing committee member's response to a questionnaire submitted to him on September 26, 1961: "I didn't answer questions . . . because I wasn't here last year. I'm not married, don't own livestock, don't own a range and I don't know which mountain you are talking about."

of an Indian Agent to let the Navajo elect a leader by utilizing the principle that the candidate receiving a majority of votes cast is declared the winner. The action took place in the Pueblo Bonito school and agency district (later named the Pueblo Bonito Agency and, more recently, the Crownpoint Subagency) under the direction of Samuel F. Stacher, the School Superintendent. The episode is recalled by John Perry, a Navajo who served as Stacher's interpreter for the occasion:

> In 1920, the Indian Agent Stacher for the Crownpoint area felt that his program suffered from a lack of centralized leadership among the Navajos. He requested that a meeting be called to elect a leader of the Navajo people, so that the Government program could be pushed by this elected leader.
>
> The meeting took place at Charley Jim's, while a Yeibichai dance was underway. This place is near the Old Dalton Trading Post. Mr. Stacher was present and I translated for him. Mr. Stacher explained the reason he wanted a leader, and how they should go about electing one. The majority principle was explained, and that each man who was nominated would be given a chance to talk before the vote was taken. Three men were nominated. The first was Casamero Tsinajinni, the second was Chief Becenti, and the third was Atsidi Yazzi Biyé. These three men all gave a talk, and the vote was taken in the following manner. The people who were in favor of Chief Becenti were asked to go over and stand near him, and the ones favoring the other two were to go and stand near them. Two of the nominated men had what seemed like an equal number of voters standing near them, and one man had but a few people standing near him.
>
> It was decided to count the fewer men around Atsidi Yazzi Biyé first, and the number was 50. Next, Stacher counted those people around Chief Becenti, then the people around Casamero Trinajinni. The count was Becenti 333 votes, and Casamero Tsinajinni got 330 votes; thus Becenti was elected as chief or headman for the people around Crownpoint by 3 votes. This was how we did things then. However, it did not change things very much as we still went to our regular leaders and did what they suggested, just as we did before Stacher had the vote, but I guess Stacher felt better. [Interview, 1962.]

It is evident that Stacher's attempt to establish a position of central authority over the people of the Pueblo Bonito jurisdiction was a failure in the mind of his interpreter, who very likely reflected the attitudes of most of the Navajos who participated in the affair. It is possible that Stacher did not know about the local political leadership pattern and was operating on the principle that he was instituting for the first time some means by which political matters could be handled. It is to Stacher's credit that, when he learned of Hunter's success, he immediately began a vigorous campaign to organize the Navajos in his jurisdiction into chapters; by 1934 Pueblo Bonito had over 25 chapters in operation. However, Stacher's first experiment in local self-government for the Crownpoint Navajos was nothing more than a beginner's class in the use of the majority rule as a means to settle a political issue.

A second instance of local political groups in action prior to the introduction of chapters is related by Howard Gorman, Council delegate from the Ganado area. Gorman recalled:

> When I returned to the reservation in 1926, after attending school, I was asked to record the minutes of several meetings held between the headmen of Ganado and Nazlini. These meetings were not held in any one place, but usually at a wedding ceremony or some other kind of ceremony such as a Squaw Dance. There were no fixed dates and no fixed topics unless it was a special meeting to settle such a thing as murder by witchcraft.
>
> The leaders in Ganado were Taayooni and Ganado Mucho's sons. They were very much like their fathers, in that Ganado Mucho's son was very mild and sought peaceful ways to settle issues; and Taayooni was hard and "angry" and wanted to take issues and do something immediately and fast. There were two leaders there, but both were wise fellows though.
>
> These leaders were selected because of their wealth, because of their clan, and because they had the ability to see what was going to happen in the future. Some of these fellows had as many as five wives, and they all were good weavers, and you know that means lots of money coming in from weaving, wool, and lambs. Taayooni was of the Totsooni clan and Ganado Mucho's son was of the Bit'ahni clan. These men had the wisdom to see what way the people should follow, thus were respected. They were headmen, and they ruled their groups, but not with force, but mildly. There were five of these types of groups with headmen in the present district 17. Each of these groups were organized and held meetings. If by chance there was a dispute between these groups, then a neutral ground was selected and the two groups got together and settled the difficulty. Such a meeting between Nazlini and Ganado was held when I was the "secretary" or recorder of the Ganado group in 1926. I wrote down the things that were decided, and thus we had a record. [Interview, 1962.]

[Gorman remembers when the chapter idea was introduced to the Navajos of Ganado.]

> Yes, I was there, and all of us thought it was a good idea, for it built upon what was already present, that of organized group meetings. Hunter's ideas added

some new things, such as the *Robert's Rules of Order,* majority voting, elected officials, and the office of chairman. We would address these elected people as "Mr. Chairman," instead of "My Elder" or *Sha Hastoui,* but the same kind of respect was meant. In the days before the chapters, we would take up all kinds of issues, such as stealing, adultery, grazing transgressions, rape, straying sheep, as well as have trials on witchcraft and the like. The headmen acted as judges, and asked for the facts, and got them too. There was no fooling around, and when he would pronounce his verdict, that was it. If he asked that a certain man or woman be present, they were brought there and the headman sat there in front of them and asked them questions in front of the crowd. Such a decision might be that the individual had to stay indoors after dark, and not to go wandering around at night, and if he did not do this, then he could expect severe punishment even death.

Later, when Hunter's chapters were organized, some of this continued in the chapter organization and some of it outside. By this, I mean that if a headman was president of a chapter then it would continue, if not it was handled by the headman outside of the chapter in the older way. [Interview, 1962.]

[In regard to the role women played in the early days of the chapter movement and how issues were settled, Gorman stated:]

The women never did have a big part in talking at a meeting, but they always voted, and since we did a lot more talking than voting the women were always in the background.

Sometimes we talked for a whole day or more on one issue, then when it came to a vote, the president pointed to one side of the room, or if we were meeting outside then to a place, and tell those who were in favor of the issue to go and stand there, and then he would point to another place and tell those who disagreed to go there and stand.

This is how we elected our chapter officers too, as each candidate would be given a place to stand, and all those people who favored that man would go and stand with him. If the vote was close then a count was made. If it was just a minor issue, the president merely called for a standing vote, and all those in favor would stand, and all those opposed sat down. This was not used outside, like in front of a trading post, for many people were already standing, so the vote was taken by separation, and each side had a place to go.

The statements from Gorman clearly indicate that, at least in the Ganado area, the Navajo readily accepted the chapter idea and incorporated such democratic features as majority rule, the right of women to vote, and techniques of European-derived parliamentary procedure within a pre-existing political organization of Navajo origin.

The chapter idea originating with Hunter in the Leupp Agency very probably built upon similar local political institutions in that area. In order to contact the Navajo leaders, Hunter stated: "I went out with an interpreter and personally contacted the headmen in the outlying areas, and also I got a lot of help from the traders in the area, for they knew who was who" (interview, 1961). Once a headman was found, Hunter related,

> I started off slow, telling a little at a time. Then as I felt the headman began to understand, I continued until I told him everything I could think of about how and the reason why I wanted them to organize a meeting. I tried to include everything, and sometimes we would spend three or four days talking to this one man, for I knew if I couldn't convince the headman, I would not have a chance in the world in getting a meeting started in that area.

A measure of Hunter's success in establishing chapters is the fact that when he left in 1928, to assume the Superintendency of the Southern Navajo Agency at Fort Defiance (see pls. 1 and 3), there were chapters at Tolchico, Sand Springs, Red Lake (Tolani), Sunrise, and Bird Spring involving about 500 Navajos of the Leupp Agency. Each chapter had three elected officers; a president (originally called "chief"), a vice-president (originally called the "vice-chief"), and a secretary, each of whom held office for one year. The five chapters were encouraged to plan such projects as building a meeting house, making roads and bridges, and beginning work on irrigation or water retention dams.

The pattern of the work projects of the first five chapters put the president of the chapter in charge, with the other officers second in command. No person was paid for his labor. In addition, the members of the chapter had to supply almost all of the building materials, wagons, dirt scoops, logs, and draft animals for the project, with the agency donating such things as nails, cement, extra feed for the draft animals, and technical assistance such as building plans and land survey equipment. The agency people were instructed by Hunter, "to keep in the background, and let the chapter president direct you and the project" (Interview, 1961).

A second chapter program was started in the Southern Navajo jurisdiction shortly after Hunter assumed the position of superintendent of that agency in 1928. To implement this program Hunter employed several field workers including: James Lowery Rush, a trader on the Navajo Reservation; Clyde Lizer, a bilingual Navajo; John Watchman, a bilingual Navajo leader from Red Lake; and Henry Gatewood, a bilingual Navajo from the Crystal area. Hunter also sought and received the support of such leaders as Chee Dodge of Crystal and Little Silversmith from the Oak Springs–Houck area. All of these men and many others helped in organizing chapters in the Southern Navajo Agency. According to J. L. Rush:

> We were told to organize "Town Meetings" among the Navajo people. But as most everybody knows, Navajos don't live in towns; and they had never heard of town meetings, elected officers, or the majority rule. However, we went out and found headmen of outfits, told them about our plans for community meetings and projects, and in almost all cases we got them interested and chapters started.
>
> The first meetings were held at crossroads, or near a trading post, but in all cases, a good supply of water was considered the most important item in the selection of a meeting place. We held these first meetings right on the ground, and everybody just gathered around and listened. [See pl. 2.] Generally, the women sat down and the men stood up, and anyone that talked usually worked his way up to the center of the group as he talked. Some of the men that did the talking got right to the point, others would wander around, and take a long time to get to the thing he wanted to say. The men did almost all of the talking, and the women only a little bit.
>
> We tried a lot of things in the early days, such as paper ballots in voting. We found out that Navajos would not say "No" to anything, so we tried voting on slips of paper, with an "X" for "Yes" and a dash [—] for "No" but it did not work, because the Navajos did not like to vote that way—did not understand this method. We also tried recording everything, writing it down, only to find that even though they voted favorably on an issue one day, they very often changed their mind in a few days and voted against it. A vote for or against an issue never meant very much; what counted was what they did about it, and then we would find out what was decided.
>
> The chapters I helped organize had four officers: a president; a vice-president; a secretary; and a person appointed to maintain order in the meeting. There were no specified terms of office for any of these officers, no badges, no symbols of office, and no pay for any of them. We tried to make sure the headmen of the area were elected as presidents of the chapters, and after that we did what Mr. Hunter told us to do, which was to "Let it Roll, Let it Roll." And sometimes, I would sit there with Clyde Lizer three and four days in a row, while the Navajo people decided what they were going to do as a project; time was not a problem to the Navajos. [Interview, 1961.]

[Rush related how a local group would go about selecting a president of a new chapter:]

> The agency never selected them, the people were given the idea and they took the idea from us about a chapter, but we did not select the leaders, they did. The agency people, like myself, were at the first meetings, and we did get the meeting going. The vote was taken by asking all those favoring "so-and-so" to stand at one side of the room, and those opposing him to stand on the other side. This was called a standing vote, and while we were aware that some people were intimidated by this technique—were afraid to be in a minority—it worked out the best for all concerned.
>
> The way it worked out was that, when we went into an area, we told them to think about who they wanted as president, and they had several weeks to think about who would be best; then, when people were nominated for president—there were usually two or three men nominated—the first one on the list got elected, for no one voted against another in those days, and the first one nominated was the one the community wanted anyway. [ibid.]

In general, the early chapter meetings were 2- or 3-day affairs, with the people of an area staying overnight in small family camps each of which supplied its own food, fuel, and shelter.

As each chapter was organized, the agency representative suggested various community projects that the new chapter might want to start. The agency person often helped them organize the membership's manpower and resources once a project had been decided upon. One of the favorite projects of chapters in the 1930's was the building of a chapter house in which they could hold meetings (see pls. 2, 3, and 10), although there were other projects that benefited the community-at-large (see pls. 3, 4, and 5), such as spring development, recreation, sewing, road making and repairing, erosion control, the building of dipping vats and corrals for livestock, and the construction of *charcos* [13] and dams. The chapter meetings were utilized by the agency personnel as a time in which they could explain what the Government was doing to help the Navajo, and as a listening post in which they could gauge the people's receptiveness to the various Government programs.

Many of the chapter houses built in the 1930's are still in use today as meeting places. Some of them were made to resemble hogans, but on a larger scale and with windows. The materials used varied with localities; they included logs, stone, and adobe. The round hoganlike chapter houses had a single room, but the rectangular structures frequently had several rooms in addition to the main meeting room. The additional rooms were used as kitchens, storerooms, and as a place where some

[13] Earthen catch basin similar to ⊔ with flaring arms; used for catching and retaining water. The face of the basin may be up to 100 yards in width.

older women could gather to listen to the discussions without being seen. Most of the chapter houses built in the early period had no modern conveniences such as toilets, electric lights, running water, or heating units, and a chapter was considered fortunate if it had a table, several chairs, benches, and all the glass windowpanes intact.

The location of the original chapter houses was usually on a road and frequently near a trading post. However, the two most important criteria used in locating a chapter house were that it be near a good supply of water (trading posts were invariably located near an adequate water supply), and near the center of the area looked upon by the people in the chapter as their home territory or land-use community. The location of a chapter house in or near the center of a land-use community is interpreted as a function of the organizational guidelines set up by Hunter, which prescribed that the leaders of the local group determine the membership area for their particular chapter. In all of the statements concerning the formation of chapters among the Navajo in the late 1920's and the early 1930's, none indicated that the agency personnel determined the membership areas of chapters, and all agreed that this matter was left entirely up to the headmen.

There is little doubt but that this principle of organization accounts in great measure for the acceptance of the chapter idea among the Navajo. The chapters were integrated into preexisting, local sociopolitical structures which had at their core the extended family structure that functioned as the basic unit of social control among the Navajo people.

The social organization of the Navajo during this period was basically the same as that which had been reinstituted after their release from Fort Sumner in 1868. The basic group that lived, moved, hunted, herded livestock, farmed, and attended ceremonials together was commonly the matrilineal, matrilocal, extended family, although not all groupings conformed to this picture (Kluckhohn and Leighton, 1946, p. 56). The members of this group most often lived close to each other in semipermanent hogan camps. The Navajos are a multiple-residence people, who move several times a year. A family group may have a permanent summer camp and a permanent winter camp with several intermediate camps between these bases. These camps are not necessarily very far apart—usually no more than 30 miles from each other. In recent years such factors as trading posts, schools, grazing districts, chapters, and tribal- or Government-built water facilities have tended to restrict mobility; yet, prior to the existence of these limiting features, the Navajos' transhumant pattern was small scale.

The formal unit that binds family groups together is the matrilineal exogamous clan, the members of which are not localized in any one area, but are segmented and appear as subunits of local groups. There are at least 60 different clans among the Navajos today, with clan members unevenly distributed over the entire area of Navajo country. It was found in a survey of 65 Navajo "communities" that a few clans predominated in each while others had only a small membership.[14] My "communities" were delimited on the basis of current chapter membership and conform only vaguely to what Kluckhohn and Leighton (1946, p. 63) have identified as a larger "outfit" which includes a hundred or more individuals who live on lands that have unbroken contiguity. Within a contemporary Navajo "community" various localities are described by informants as "the place where Bitter Water people live," or "around here Red Streak in the Water people live." The existence of these fractionated or segmented portions of a clan in specific areas within a Navajo land-use community is partially determined by the observance of a matrilocal pattern of residence and a tendency for certain clans to become affiliated by marriage (Carr, Spencer, and Woolley, 1939, p. 245). The members of a segmented clan in a local area expect mutual aid and cooperation from each other in all aspects of social and economic life; even though a man moves away from his family of orientation, he is expected to honor his duty and responsibility toward his sister and her children. Traditionally, a niece expected to inherit a small amount of property from each of her maternal uncles and, in turn, was expected to offer shelter, food, and other economic necessities in the event her maternal uncles were in need. It is thought that the clans in Navajo culture were the supreme unit of social control and that each member of a clan was responsible for the actions and behavior of his clan brothers and sisters (Collier, 1951, p. 12).

Whatever social control a clan once had over its members in traditional Navajo culture, it still is a potent force in the social life of most Navajos today. For example: clan exogamy regulates the selection of marriage partners; clan affiliation is frequently given instead of personal names when Navajos who are strangers first meet; and, in the political arena, council delegates who vote against their clan brothers are accused openly of being "disloyal." Political action on the local "community" level demands that a person be supported by his fellow clansmen and those of related clans on election day; usually the clan segment that has the most elects one of their own as headman, grazing committeeman, Council delegate, or chapter officer. For a clansman to do otherwise would jeopardize his social and economic life, especially in that most of the voting on the local level is done on a standing or sitting basis in full view of all.

The clan-affiliation basis of chapter membership was

[14] Unpublished results of a survey of Navajo "communities," conducted by me in 1962.

occasionally broken and a "newcomer" was allowed to become a chapter member; for example the spouse of a member was included with full rights both to vote and to be considered for an office of the chapter. The traditional residence pattern among Navajos after marriage was matrilocal and the prospective new members were most often males. However, mere residence in an area did not allow new members of the land-use community the right to be included as members of a chapter, as this depended upon many years of residence, good behavior, and wise counsel to those who sought them out for advice. Thus a man might become a member of his wife's chapter after 10 to 15 years residence with his family of procreation. Statements on this matter indicate that a person's chances of becoming a member of a spouse's chapter increased in proportion to the number of clan members of his own who were indigenous to the area: if a man born into the Bitter Water clan moved upon marriage to an area in which there were many Bitter Water clan members, his chances of attaining chapter membership were much greater than those of a man whose clan had fewer members in an area.

In the early years of the chapter movement, the primary function of the chapters was to act as the political organization of the land-use community, which was composed of various groups of people united by a common cultural tradition but divided on the local level due to the existence of exogamous matrilineal clans. The clans with the greatest number of members generally exercised the greatest amount of social control over the entire population of the land-use community. Estimates vary as to the population of these land-use communities, but in general they seem to have included about 500 people. The introduction of the chapter provided a means by which community-wide decisions could be settled and a means by which the community-at-large could cooperate on common projects. The chapters also provided a formal communication link between the local groups and the Government Indian Agents where none had existed before. The chapters pulled together the various divided elements within the land-use community and provided a means by which these various groups could work together for common goals. For many years prior to the introduction of the chapter, land-use communities settled these issues at large ceremonial gatherings such as the Night Chant, Squaw Dance, and Yeibichai. However, as the Navajo became more involved in the Government's program of directed change, the large ceremonial gathering probably did not serve the new political needs of the people. At these ceremonials there was only casual contact with the Indian Agents, and no regular channels of communication between local groups and the agents directing the culture change. There was, no doubt, an earnest desire among many Navajos to know what the Indian agency had to offer them as individuals and as members of a community. The chapters provided a two-way communication channel that benefited both the Navajos and the Indian Agents.

There was no attempt to link the various chapters, in the first years of their existence, with the Council delegates or the Navajo Tribal Council. When the Soil Conservation Service set up the land management districts, however, they worked through the chapters in establishing the subunits which later became the precincts that elected members to the reorganzied Council in 1936. During the period of voluntary stock reduction the chapters "were the backbone of the program" (Henry Smith interview, 1961). However, when stock were forcibly reduced—starting with horses in 1937, and later including sheep in 1943—the chapters became the centers of resistance to the program, and Government support was withdrawn from the chapters. The Superintendent of the Navajo Service during the stock reduction period stated:

> There was not a conscious effort to destroy the chapters on the Navajo Reservation. However, I was interested in the creation of a *Tribe* and I felt the chapters tended to maintain provincialism and isolation. Thus, I hoped to increase the strength and influence of the Navajo Tribal Council which could act for the Navajo people as a tribe. [E. R. Fryer interview, 1962.]

A number of chapters ceased to function when Government support was withdrawn, and the number of active chapters was reduced from about 80 in 1937 to 40 in 1943.

The rise and decline of the chapters in Navajo country is seen by Robert Young, Indian Affairs Officer of the Gallup Area office of the Bureau of Indian Affairs, as related to the stock reduction program, but not exclusively as a result of it:

> The chapters during the period of 1933 to 1934 were used as centers for the Soil Conservation people, range-riders, and district supervisors to inform the Navajo people about the stock adjustment. Grazing permits were set up in terms of the chapters and their membership areas. It is wrong to think of the chapters as diminishing during the 1930's; for, if anything, the stock adjustment program strengthened their program, for it allowed a place for the people to discuss and cuss the Government program. There were forums, and much of the discussion was done by former students. These students were the Navajos that had gone off to school, when it was not very popular as it is today. These men, then young, were informed and could read the regulations, and understood what was involved in the stock adjustment. Now, these men, today, still get

blamed for the success of the stock adjustment program, but they were the leaders in the discussions.

The chapters declined, but only after 1937, and then . . . , only a few. After 1943, there was a general decline, but that was after the forced reduction of sheep and goats. On the other hand, the schools became centers of community interest during the late 1930's and continued to occupy this central position until the chapter program by the Navajo Tribal Council was initiated in 1952. There was also the Returned Students Association that operated within the chapter organization, as well as Livestock Growers Association that was begun in the early 1930's . . . and these groups tried to influence Navajos to adjust their livestock, and advised their people to seek alternatives to the subsistence dependency on sheep. [Interview, 1962.]

The shift of community interest from chapters to schools in many localities was one aspect of the general sociocultural change among Navajos during the 1930's and 1940's. Statements from informants concerning the participation of Navajos in chapter organizations during this period strongly indicates that the elders, the *Sha Hastoui,* in many cases ceased to take an active leadership role within the local chapters, and that many women stopped attending the meetings. The primary cause for this nonparticipation was the role chapter officers played in assisting the Government's stock reduction program. As the informants pointed out, the chapter leaders were enforcing the stock quotas at the expense of the small stock owners while keeping their own herds in prime condition.

The voluntary program of stock reduction placed the responsibility of maintaining the stock quotas for each locality on the chapter in that area. The quotas for various localities were arrived at by conferences on the grazing district level, with the district supervisor, the rangeriders, and the Council delegates in attendance. These quotas were then made the responsibility of the chapters in areas where they existed, and the land management district supervisor held the chapter officers responsible for maintaining these quotas. The chapter officers, in turn, passed this responsibility on down to the various extended families within the chapter membership area, and assigned each family group the number of sheep units they were to maintain.

The heaviest burden of the voluntary stock reduction program was borne by the small stock owners, who also comprised those groups that were frequently less politically powerful and had less prestige and less numerical strength in the local chapter area. Two methods were employed by the chapter leaders to maintain livestock quotas on the local level under the voluntary reduction program.

The first method was used in the event the district supervisor decided a chapter area had to reduce its total number of livestock by so many units; the chapter officers assigned each family in the area a specified number of sheep to be contributed to the total. Usually the number of sheep units contributed to the total by each family was equal: for example, if 100 families in an area were required to contribute 500 sheep, each family would be required to give up 5 sheep, regardless of the size of the family's herd. This method hit the family with small flocks harder than it did the ones with large herds.

The second method involved the assignment of a specified number of sheep units per family on the basis of productive capacity of the pastures used by the individual families. Thus, the less productive pastures had the number of sheep units on them reduced, and these pastures were most frequently used by poorer groups of people in a chapter area. In addition, the poorer groups of Navajos in chapter areas were often divided into a greater number of different clans and clan segments than the wealthier, politically powerful clan segments who normally controlled the best grazing lands in a chapter area. Under either method of voluntary livestock reduction, therefore, a few clan segments with their greater wealth in sheep and pasture and greater numerical strength were able to maintain a superior position at the expense of those clan segments which composed the minority. In part this was due to a traditional culture pattern among the Navajo that prescribed that members of the same clan were expected to do no less than protect the other members of their clan, and to support them in all social, economic, and political matters.

The stock reduction program was clearly a success in terms of reducing the actual number of sheep, goats, and horses maintained by the Navajo, but the economic position of the small livestock holder became serious by 1940, because they continued to bear the major share of the voluntary stock reduction program. These people began to stay away from the chapter meetings and to employ negative sanctions against the leaders of the chapters who were, by and large, the big stock owners. These negative sanctions included gossip, ridicule, and accusations of witchcraft. Kluckhohn's systematic analysis of witchcraft imagery among the Navajo documents that

> at various crucial times in the history of the Navajo, clever leaders have used the accusation of witchcraft as an effective means of social control . . . . Thus, during the last difficult years of controversy over the stock reduction program, there has been appreciably more witchcraft excitement than for sometime past. [Kluckhohn, 1944, p. 120.]

[The differential participation of those Navajos accused of witchcraft within the general social life of the Navajo is analyzed by Kluckhohn, to whom]

> . . . a total of 222 cases of persons accused of witchcraft . . . was available. . . . One hundred and eighty-four were men; all were adults. . . . All women accused were definitely old; 131 of the men were definitely old (spoken of as "old", "very old," "greyhaired," "whitehaired," etc.). One hundred and forty of the men were described as ceremonial practitioners of some sort, but it must be remembered that the proportion of adult Navajo men who are ceremonial practitioners is very high. Twenty-one of the men were said to be "headmen" or "chiefs." This is an exceedingly high figure, considering the proportion of such leaders to the total adult male population. . . . One hundred and fifteen out of the total group were described as rich or "well-off"; 17 were described as poor or very poor; for the remainder no economic information was available. [Ibid., p. 59.]

These figures support the inference that the negative sanctions employed against the wealthier and more politically powerful local group leaders (who were frequently the chapter officers) had the effect of removing them from active roles in general chapter matters and specifically terminating their official role as enforcement officers in the stock reduction program. As these local leaders withdrew from chapter activities, many units foundered and failed. The failure of nearly half of the chapters in Navajo country during the last few years of the 1930's and the first years of the next decade can be attributed in great measure to the loss of faith in the land-use community leaders who led the chapter organization, and there was a general retreat to the older more traditional pattern; that of looking to one's own clan elder for political, social, and economic leadership.

Data collected from 65 communities in 1962, indicate that those communities in which chapters continued to operate had either a more diversified economic base (farming, wagework, livestock) with the resultant lack of exclusive dependence upon livestock raising, or a chapter membership area which included five or six local clan segments of nearly equal numerical strength and a more equitable distribution of wealth in the form of livestock among the chapter membership. Thus, it seems that in those Navajo land-use communities where the chapter was used by the one or two numerically superior, wealthy clan segments to further extend their socioeconomic control over the rest of the local population, the chapter organization disintegrated when the leaders of these clans ceased to participate in positions of leadership. In other land-use communities—where there was a more equitable distribution of wealth and population among the various clan segments within the area—the chapters continued to function, even though the positions of leadership changed hands. The fact is that at least 40 chapters succeeded in maintaining a semblance of an organization from the time they were first organized in 1930 to the present; even though the number of meetings held during the 1940's dropped drastically from that during the 1930's the structure has remained essentially intact.

The overall function of the chapters has changed and adapted to other sociopolitical changes in the life of the Navajo people. In the beginning, the chapter served as a more efficient communication link between the Government agencies and the Navajo, and as a means by which the staff of the Bureau of Indian Affairs could influence the Navajo to engage in self-help community projects. It provided the people with a local political organization which they could use to express their opinions about the various Government programs initiated for their benefit, and provided the local Navajo land-use community with a formal structure for a set of informal intermittent political activities already functioning in Navajo culture.

The chapters functioned during the stock reduction program of the late 1930's and early 1940's both as political forums and as active participants in helping the Government reduce the number of livestock on Navajo ranges. Many chapters disintegrated and dissolved because their leaders imposed too heavy a burden on the small stock holders who ceased to participate in chapter activities and who employed traditional Navajo negative sanctions against these leaders, causing many of them to resign their offices. Under these circumstances many chapters lacked solid community support and the meetings stopped being held; the chapters lay dormant until 1955, when they were reactivated by the Navajo Tribal Council.

NAVAJO TRIBAL CHAPTERS

The Navajo Tribal Council officially recognized and set in motion certification of chapters by passing on June 20, 1955, the Navajo Tribal Resolution CJ–20–55, which was approved by the Secretary of the Interior's office on August 12, 1955. The Preamble of this resolution states:

> WHEREAS: 1. For more than 20 years the chapter system on the Navajo Reservation has met an urgent need

of Navajo communities in providing a medium of the dissemination of information, a center for local planning and discussion, and a ready agency for the mediation of local disputes, and

2. It is the intention of the Navajo Tribe to give official recognition and status to the local chapters in the Tribal Constitution itself, to continue the valuable functions set forth in (1) above and to constitute a 'grassroots' foundation for the Navajo Tribal Government, and

3. Pending adoption of the proposed tribal constitution and fuller definition of the status, function and powers of the local chapters, it is the desire of the Navajo Tribe to encourage and foster these community organizations to the greatest extent possible.

[The Resolution also provided:]

It is the intent of the Navajo Tribal Council to encourage the regular functioning of one (1) chapter organization in each of the 74 election communities and, at the present time, the Council does not favor the operation of more than one chapter in any one election community. However, in those few localities where more than one chapter remains active in an election community, both are hereby authorized to apply for certification and provided in (c) subject to later determination of the Council as to continuation of such additional chapter.

The official sanctions bestowed upon the chapters by the Navajo Tribal Council as a "grassroots" element in tribal government has strengthened their position as the local political government for the majority of the Navajo people. The official recognition also put an end to speculations that the chapters would eventually die out, as they were "entirely artificial" (Kluckhohn and Leighton, 1946, p. 101), or that "an artificial system like the chapters had vitality only so long as it was subsidized by the government. When that subsidy was withdrawn, they collapsed. The reason for the collapse can be attributed to the fact that Navajos with the power and prestige took little active part and the chapters were foreign to Navajo thinking and experience." (Kimball and Provinse, 1942, p. 24.) However, by 1950 a number of Navajo authorities had changed their minds about the persistence of chapters: Van Valkenburgh, who had earlier described them as "loose and rather comical forms of parliamentary regulations" (1945, p. 73), felt that, in 1955, they served the needs of individuals rather than groups (in Shepardson, 1963, p. 84). Solon Kimball agreed, and said the ". . . fact that they have life shows that they fulfill a local need intermediate between the Tribal Council and the people, perhaps as a transition organization from an older Navajo pattern" (1950, p. 23). A number of studies have been made of chapter activities in the 1950's which attest to the vitality and flexibility of these local political units of the Navajo (Bunker, 1956; Green, 1957; Rapoport, 1954; Sasaki, 1960; Shepardson, 1963).

At the time the chapters were officially recognized by the Navajo Tribal Council, it set forth rules of certification. The Resolution CJ–20–55 stated that there was to be at least one chapter organization in each precinct which elected a delegate to the Council. In some precincts there were several active chapters, and each was given official status. Any new chapters, however, were to be certified only after they had received the approval of the advisory, and budget and finance committees of the Council. A new chapter was required to present evidence that they represented a group which had existed and functioned as a community for many years. This point was relatively easily established for many local groups, especially if they had had an earlier chapter organization that had dissolved during the early 1940's. A new chapter had to present evidence that the population of an area exceeded 1,000 persons for each of the existing chapters, thus indicating there was a need to establish others; or (in cases where a local group was not able to present evidence of sufficient population) the topography of the area was such that travel to the present chapter area was extremely difficult and physically dangerous many months of the year, thus not allowing the petitioners to attend the existing chapter meeting. Therefore, if a group of people were cut off by canyons, or stretches of desert or mountains, they were allowed to form a chapter even though the existing chapter membership was below 1,000 in number. In no case was the number of chapters in Navajo country to exceed 96 units.

The various political positions and titles within the earlier chapter structure were retained by the Resolution with the stipulation that each chapter officer was elected to serve a 4-year term. The Resolution did not provide for such circumstances as resignation, death, recall, and reelection of chapter officers. This resulted in considerable confusion until the advisory committee passed Resolution ACO–149–59 on October 2, 1959, which set forth a number of procedures for the election of chapter officers, and described the duties and responsibilities of each officer of a chapter. The advisory committee requested each chapter membership to have read aloud, in English and Navajo, the rules outlined in the 1959 resolution, and to vote on whether or not these rules were acceptable (see Appendix).

The 1959 rules allowed all of the chapter officers a vote in all chapter elections, and a plurality vote elected each officer. The 4-year term of office for each officer was to begin on July 1st of a tribal election year, and in the event of death, disability, resignation, removal of an officer from the community, or ineligibility of an officer, an election was to be held for the remaining portion of the 4-year term. There was no limit to the number of successive terms a person could serve as a chapter officer. Any officer of a chapter could be removed from his position upon the presentation of a written petition signed by at least 20 adult members of the chapter, and an election was required to fill the vacancy. The chapter officer removed by a recall petiton had the right to stand for reelection, if he so desired.

In general the duties of each officer, as described by ACO–149–59, are:

President. The president shall preside at all meetings, have power to call meetings with consent of the other officers, attend tribal meetings and represent the chapter as called upon to do so. He shall have a vote in all chapter elections.

Vice-President. The vice-president shall perform the duties of the president in case of disability or absence of the president, and shall have a vote in chapter elections.

Secretary. The secretary shall prepare written minutes or reports of all meetings, carry on correspondence, and act as treasurer of chapter funds. He shall have a vote in chapter elections.

The manner of electing chapter officers by a standing vote was retained, and a quorum for an election meeting was defined as at least 25 adult members over 21 years of age. Nominations for the various chapter offices did not require a second, and all nominations were to be completed for all vacant offices before any voting took place. Any person was eligible to hold a chapter office except an elected delegate to the Navajo Tribal Council.

The chapters were given additional support by the Navajo Tribal Council through the appropriation of funds to pay chapter officers a per diem allowance of $12 (subsequently changed to $17) provided they attended and served in their elected capacity as the officers of the chapter meetings. The chapter presidents were allowed the rate of $17 a day, plus mileage to and from their homes at the rate of 10 cents per mile, for attendance at an annual 3-day meeting of chapter presidents to be called by the chairman of the Tribal Council and to be held at Window Rock, Arizona.

Each chapter was allowed to hold two meetings a month (changed in 1960 to three meetings a month), for which its officers could claim compensation, and they were required to hold at least 12 meetings a year to remain eligible for continuing recognition and payments in a succeeding year. The chapter secretary was required to submit report forms which were used as a basis for the payment of the officers. These forms are almost always carried by hand to Window Rock by one of the chapter officers, and a system has been devised to have the claims paid on the day they are submitted, so that the chapter officer bringing the claims can return to his home community that same day with the per diem pay for himself and the other chapter officers. However, since the payments are made by check, a trip to a town off the reservation is usually made, rather than returning home and letting the local trading post cash the tribal check. This set of linkages and others are discussed subsequently in regard to the tribal agency coordinating the current chapter program.

A building program initiated by the Navajo Tribe was begun in the mid-1950's, and many new chapter houses were constructed. By 1962, there were over 50 modern buildings serving as meeting places for chapters, all of which were built from funds supplied by the Navajo Tribe. The new chapter units cost from $40,000 to over $100,000 each. The main source of tribal money came from the production of oil and gas deposits on reservation land. Table 1 shows the amount of income from these sources over a 10-year period. These figures show a considerable increase in tribal income for the period 1957–60 over the 1951–56 period. Since 1958 a total of over $4,000,000 has been spent on building new and remodeling older chapter houses.

TABLE 1.—*Navajo tribal income from oil and gas: 1951–60*[1]

Year	Income	Year	Income
1951	$1, 245, 278	1957	$34, 807, 982
1952	1, 428, 546	1958	29, 194, 756
1953	5, 161, 912	1959	15, 323, 947
1954	5, 310, 201	1960	11, 688, 646
1955	1, 544, 061		
1956	1, 479, 697	Total	$107, 185, 026

[1] Young, 1961, p. 269.

The chapter program was further strengthened by the creation of the Community Services Department (later called the Community Development Department) designed to coordinate chapter affairs for all of the 96 units and responsible for developing and administering community services for the benefit of the Navajo (Council Resolution CJ–10–57). At present the Community Development Department functions as one of the units under the Public Services Division (see fig. 1, p. 27) and the organizational link between the 96 chapters and other tribal bureaus; for example, it approves per diem allowances for all chapter officers. The Director of the Community Development Department oversees the work of five fieldworkers, who visit and assist the chapters at least four out of five working days. Contact is maintained between the chapters and tribal personnel in two major ways: by frequent visits of chapter officers to the tribal offices at Window Rock to have their per diem vouchers approved; and by visits of Community Development fieldworkers. In addition to these formal arrangements, chapters almost always have one or more visitors attending each of the 96 chapter meetings held three times a month.

The new chapter buildings are modern structures (see pls. 7–9), and most of them have such fixtures as running water, electricity, and butane heating. Each new chapter house has a modern kitchen (no refrigerator), an office, and a large meeting hall. Many of the new chapter buildings have restrooms for men and women, showers, sewing rooms with machines, craft rooms, and a laundry room complete with hot water, tubs, and electric washing machines. The labor required to build these new chapter houses has been recruited from local sources whenever possible. The buildings are designed by registered architects, and the actual construction is supervised by the Design and Construction Department of the Navajo Tribe.

Chapter meetings are held about every 10 days. While there is no tribal-wide schedule of dates for these meetings, they are usually held on Saturday or Sunday, with Sunday as the most popular meeting day. Notices of meetings are posted in public places in the chapter area, at the local trading posts, and are published occasionally in the *Navajo Times*—a weekly newspaper owned and operated by the Navajo Tribe. Meetings also are announced over the radio on programs sponsored by the Navajo Tribe along with other news of interest to the Navajo in their own language. The news of a meeting of a local chapter is also spread by word-of-mouth, and interest in attending is increased if a chapter election is planned or a high ranking tribal official is scheduled to address the local meetng. In general, it was observed that there were two peak periods of attendance during a year's period; early spring, and late fall before the heavy snows.[15]

Most frequently, the notices stated that the chapter meetings were to start at 10 o'clock in the morning; however, the pattern observed was that they started about noon and lasted until dusk the same day. The actual meeting was begun with little fanfare by the chapter president, and his usual expression was, "I guess we have enough here to start." In none of the meetings attended was a rapping of order ever observed. The general pattern is for the three chapter officers to gather at the front of the crowd if the meeting is held out of doors and to begin to look around at the people. The president then begins by reading or telling in a soft voice about the agenda of the meeting; usually the people are relatively settled by the time the president finishes. The agenda is then handed to the secretary, and the first order of business is launched by the president.

Most chapter meetings are held indoors today, and the people sit on benches or folding chairs facing one end of the meeting hall. The most frequent arrangement observed consisted of a table with five or six chairs placed at the north end of the meeting hall.[16] From this location the chapter officers, distinguished men of the community, and visitors sat and faced the general audience. The distance between the front row of seats for the general public and the presiding officers was usually about 15 feet. Spread around in a semicircular manner from the table, toward the southeast and southwest, were chairs and benches for lesser dignitaries and less important guests. It was possible, by observing the seating arrangements, to obtain a general idea of how the particular chapter officers regarded guests and visitors at a meeting, as well as who was considered an informal leader in the community. Observations on rank of the visitors were verifiable by noting two other aspects of the meeting. The usual pattern of a meeting was to allow the guests the opportunity to speak at the beginning of a meeting; the most distinguished and the highest ranking visitor being asked to speak first, with those of less rank following. The second indication of rank order of visitors was the amount of noise or commotion during a guest's talk. If there was considerable moving about, shuffling of feet and chairs, talking, babies crying, etc., then the visitor did not rate very high in the estimation of the chapter membership. However, if babies were shushed, little boys and girls pulled down and seated, little talking or whispering done while the person spoke, this could be taken as evidence that the people in the community regarded the visitor with considerable respect and accorded him high rank especially if a visitor was asked to speak as the first or second order of chapter business. These actions of the chapter officers and the general assembly of the chapter had the function of identifying strangers in their midst; they served the dual purpose of letting the visitor know where he stood in the eyes of this particular segment of Navajo people, and exhibited the president's knowledge of the rank and prestige of nonlocal people.

There was a tendency for the women to seat themselves to the left of the chapter officers' table. In general, women and men sat in separate groups, with the former having the responsibility for the younger children. Teen-age boys stood around the fringes of the assembled group and the teen-age girls sat in groups of twos and threes with the women. The front row of chairs or benches frequently was occupied by older men, all of whom kept their hats on except when Christian prayer was offered at the beginning of a meeting. However, an invocation was commonly practiced only in the eastern area of the Navajo country and was nonexistent in most of the western chapter meetings.

[15] I attended 142 meetings over period of 18 months.

[16] With one exception, all chapter houses were built so that the main entrance faced east (one of the four sacred directions, and the direction toward which the entrance of a traditional Navajo hogan, sheep corral, and a modern outhouse face).

The group of men who form the semicircle at the front of the meeting are the main participants in the discussion undertaken by a chapter. These men are the elders of the community, and they are the ones who are called upon at ceremonials to speak. This group of men normally includes members of the district grazing committee, past and present chapter officers and Tribal Council delegates, visitors, and the respected older men of the chapter area who, if called upon to speak, often extol the virtues of the traditional Navajo way of life. The function of this group is as a council of elders whose talks are listened to with respect, and whose voting actions set the pattern for the group as a whole.

The president of a chapter acts as an administrative officer for this "inner council" and is careful to use the talents of the council at the proper times during the meeting, or suffer the risk of being called "authoritarian" or "power hungry" by the entire chapter membership. The chapter president is expected to call upon or recognize an elder versed in mythology if an action needs supernatural sanctions; to help gauge the effect of the first elder's statement of the mythology, the president might then recognize as the next speaker an elder of the most populous clan segment in the chapter area. At times the entire informal council of elders participates in a discussion, with several of its members speaking two or three times on each issue. In any chapter discussion many people of the general membership are allowed to voice their opinions. The function of the chapter president is to assist the community in formulating a consensus (opinion) of an issue. A successful president is one who guides his group's discussion of issues without leading them toward a conclusion by authoritarian methods.

The ideal decision-making pattern of Navajo chapter memberships is to discuss an issue until a consensus is reached. Frequently, the real pattern involves nearly endless discussion and debate with postponement of voting until everyone included in the chapter membership agrees. There are instances of a chapter spending over 3 years discussing an issue without resolving it. The Twin Lakes Chapter spent 4 years (1958–1962) discussing the installation of a low-pressure water system for the hogans in their community. The U.S. Public Health Service allotted about $20,000 for this project in Twin Lakes, but 4 years after the project had been approved by the U.S. Public Health Service, the Community Development Department, and the Design and Construction Department of the Navajo Tribe, the chapter membership was unwilling to give their approval because some members of this community still found the project questionable. In a Twin Lakes Chapter meeting on March 11, 1962, an older woman got up and said:

> We have been discussing this water project for more than 3 years, and always we have come around to the center of whether or not this thing is good for us, as it might change our life too much. Some say it would not affect our way of life, but I say that this is the way Pueblo people live, such as the Hopi, who are not Navajos but Pueblos. Also, I say, that since not all people in Twin Lakes will get water piped to their hogans, this will make classes of people among us, and I say the visitors here are trying to put something over on us, and divide us, and this is not good Navajo way. I say let's thank the visitors and let them go home.

The Twin Lakes community is the home area of Jacob Morgan who was very active in resisting the stock reduction program through 1937. While Jacob Morgan cooperated with the Government program after he was elected tribal chairman in 1938, many of the members of the 1962 Twin Lakes community remained opposed to any outside influence. The statement of the older Navajo woman is typical of many other statements found in the written reports submitted by the secretary of the Twin Lakes Chapter over a 4-year period. The records indicate that many other topics were taken up and resolved, but this particular issue remained unsettled. The major difficulty was that only about one-half of the membership of the chapter was to receive the benefits of this water system, and the group that was not to receive piped water to their hogans consistently blocked the efforts of those who wanted to obtain chapter approval. The core of the problem was that almost everyone in the chapter thought the U.S. Public Health Service had given the money to the community, and that the community had the right to do what it wanted to with these funds. There were frequent suggestions in the reports that the "water money" be used in some other way that would benefit the entire population of the chapter area.

The chapter president of Twin Lakes was aware of the dissatisfaction and had tried hard to bring about a feeling of unity, but with no success. He had not allowed the Twin Lakes Chapter membership to vote on this issue during the past 4 years for, even though he might have obtained a majority vote for approval, this would not have resolved the issue; anything short of a near unanimous vote has little meaning to most of the chapter memberships throughout Navajo country. The chapter president was probably aware that many of his members felt confident that if they waited long enough the U.S. Public Health Service might add additional sums of money to that already allotted to the Twin Lakes' project, so that every hogan in the community could have piped water.

The fieldman of the U.S. Public Health Service stated that they were reluctant to withdraw the funds, because it was felt that eventually the community would come to terms and accept the low-pressure water system even though it involved only a limited number of households in the Twin Lakes Chapter area. Several departments of the Navajo Tribe were anxious to help in any way possible, but were on guard lest they be accused of forcing the community to accept the proposal of the U.S. Public Health Service.

The actions of the various tribal and nontribal agencies at the Twin Lakes gathering described below illustrate the attempt most agencies make to create a neutral or nonthreatening image of their organization when they deal with Navajos on the local level. At the beginning of the meeting on March 11, 1962, the director of the Community Development Department, a Navajo, was asked to interpret for the meeting because several of the visitors were Anglos and were not able to understand Navajo, the language used in every chapter meeting all over Navajo country. The director agreed to perform this task, but asked the group to vote on whether or not his translation would be acceptable to everyone present. A vote was taken and the director was given unanimous approval to translate for the group. He said later: "If I had not been given unanimous approval to translate, I would have refused to do the job, and I would have left the meeting and gone home because I would have been accused of trying to push something off on those people."

The Design and Construction Department Director, an Anglo, told the Twin Lakes gathering that he was there only to explain that the Navajo Tribe stood ready to help them if they decided to approve the project. The help he offered was the digging of ditches from the main water pipes to the individual hogans. The director of this tribal agency told them this would be done at no charge to the hogan owners, and he wanted them to know that the Navajo Tribe stood behind them no matter what they decided. The U.S. Public Health Service field representative exerted a little more pressure by suggesting that the Twin Lakes Chapter had had 4 years in which to decide whether or not to accept this water system and, if they did not decide soon, the money might be allotted to another community. The chapter president's reaction to this last statement was to thank the visitors for coming to the meeting and to tell them they were free to leave and return to their homes. The Twin Lakes Chapter meeting on March 11, 1962, ended without taking action on the water project.

The role of the Community Development Department as a tribal-wide agency is neither neutral nor passive, for it is in the process of transforming the Navajo chapters from a town meeting type of gathering dominated by political consideration to one that serves as a local agency for social and cultural change. To do this job, the Community Development Department employs five fieldworkers who travel almost constantly from one chapter meeting to another, four and five days a week. These men help chapter members write letters, reports, and petitions to those agencies seeking to help the Navajo. The fieldworkers help the chapter officers establish bank accounts for their chapter funds. The fieldworkers suggest ways in which a chapter can raise money to finance the operation of their chapter. The suggestions include: bingo parties; movies; social dances; selling popcorn, soda pop, and candy at movies; serving meals during the chapter meetings; and charging a small fee for the use of washing machines, showers in the newer chapter buildings, power equipment, welding equipment, sewing machines, and other equipment owned jointly by the chapter organization. Many chapters have acted upon the suggestion of the fieldworkers that a fee of 50 to 75 cents be charged to guests who wish to use the facilities of the chapter house overnight (no beds are provided, only the floor, roof and walls).

The work of the fieldmen is directed by the head of the Community Development Department who, in turn, is supervised by the director of the Public Services Division of the Navajo Tribe. The administrative duties of the current director of the Community Development Department, a Navajo man with an A.B. degree from an accredited college, include such diverse tasks as justifying budgetary requests before the Navajo Tribal Council, explaining to a chapter house custodian how to light a butane-fired furnace, explaining to chapter officers that the money collected by the sale of candy and soda pop at the chapter house must not be used by them for their personal needs, and arranging for several medicine men to perform Blessing Way rites as part of the dedicatory services of a new chapter house (see pl. 8).

The equipment that the Navajo Tribe buys to furnish the new chapter houses is selected by the Community Development Department and the items secured include diesel power plants, butane kitchen stoves, dishes, knives, forks, spoons, sewing machines, toilet tissue, soap, public address systems, movie projectors, popcorn making machines, chairs, tables, typewriters, blackboards, photographs, washing machines, and American flags. The director of the Community Development Department has organized a program of culture change. He has oriented his program of community development around the concept that a change in a group's material culture will bring about a change in cultural behavior.

An elemental feature of the tribe's community development program is the installation of a modern chapter house in a community which allows the people of an area to see, use, and experience many new items of a material nature. The tribal leaders hope that in time many of the Navajos will become familiar with such things as cement floors, running water, butane stoves, windows, electricity, chairs and tables, and subsequently want these features in their own homes. The newness of the modern building with its heated water for washing cloths, showers, and the windows and electricity become less "dangerous" to the traditional Navajos who attend chapter meetings, and passive inaction in regard to these modern conveniences often changes to active participation and acceptance of their utility (Kluckhohn and Leighton, 1946, p. 226). A modern chapter house accomplishes the job of introducing to local groups of Navajos a vast array of new cultural materials, yet allows each person to accept or reject these new material items according to his personal inclinations.

To many Navajos the $50,000 chapter houses with their modern equipment stand as symbols of tribal unity, optimism, and prosperity. The chapter houses are a gift to a community from the Navajo Tribe. The tribe has the plans for chapter houses drawn by registered architects, and the tribe attempts to employ many local Navajos as workmen during the period of construction (see pls. 6 and 7). The money for a chapter house dedication comes from the tribal contingency fund, and many tribal officials attend and make speeches (pls. 6 and 9). A chapter house dedication is a gala affair with upwards of 1,000 people attending, having arrived on cradleboards, by foot, on horse, in wagons, pickup trucks, buses, cars, and airplanes. The main participants in a chapter dedication are the chapter officers, distinguished medicine men, members of the tribal band, Council delegates, Bureau of Indian Affairs personnel, tribal employes, and the local Navajo women who cook mutton stew, "fry bread," and coffee for everyone.

A chapter house dedication is usually officially started by having one or more medicine men perform a portion of the Blessing Way Ceremony for a hogan (pl. 8) and, during the ritual, corn pollen is sprinkled over the door lintels and the crowd in attendance. It is thrown in the direction of the four cardinal points beginning with the east, then the south, then the west, and ending at the north. A Christian prayer is often given as the next part of a dedication ceremony, followed by the raising of an American flag (pl. 9) by either a group of ex-military men in their wartime dress uniforms, or by the Navajo tribal police with the assistance of the local contingent of Boy Scouts. The American flag is raised as the National anthem is played by the Navajo tribal band, and some spectactors remove their hats or put a hand to their chests. Speeches are made by tribal officials, chapter officers, Council delegates, and other visitors after the flag raising ceremony. A 'keynote' speech is programmed for mid-afternoon after everyone has eaten. Frequently the speeches are translated from Navajo to English for the benefit of the Anglo visitors, and at times the talks are tape recorded for later broadcast over the radio station KGAK of Gallup, N. Mex., on the program, "The Navajo Hour," which is sponsored by the Navajo Tribe. The talks by visitors are usually interrupted (except for the distinguished guests) and stopped by the announcement that food is now being served. Long lines of people form, and many Navajos come prepared with their own dishes and coffee mugs. After everyone has been fed, the tribal band plays and the speeches are resumed. Frequently, chapter house dedications include games of skill and strength such as the Chicken Pull (without real chickens), and teams of men and women compete in Tug of War. By late afternoon, many people start home, and by nightfall only the women of the community who started cooking and preparing food 3 or 4 days before the dedication are to be found at the new chapter house cleaning up the debris and putting things in order for the first meeting.

Chapter meetings are held three or four times a month. There is no regular date for meetings to be held, but the two most frequent days are Saturday and Sunday. The rest of the week, most chapter houses are locked up and not used. The locations of the new chapter houses have followed the pattern set earlier, which was to locate near a supply of water and on a road. Due to the scattered isolated residence pattern of Navajos, the chapter houses are frequently found in remote spots, with only two or three hogans or a trading post within sight. Telephone communication with the chapters is nonexistent, and mail service is generally handled informally by the trading post in the area. In emergencies, the two-way radio system of the Navajo police can be used, if a patrol wagon is in the area. Although some chapters are equipped with television sets and radios, the major portion of communication is handled on a face-to-face basis.

The 40 chapters listed in Table 2 are located in all parts of Navajo country, and for this reason are believed to represent the 96 chapters. The percentage of members who attend the meetings varies from less than 5 percent (Twin Lakes) to as high as 36 percent (Coal Mine Mesa). The chapter at Klagetoh has an average turnout of one-third of the membership per meetings. The average attendance for the 40 chapters is about 11 percent of the memberships. The 11 percent average attendance for chapter members can be attributed to various causes: a lack of interest; the feeling that the chapters constitute old peoples' social clubs; or the fear of supernatural contamination because strangers are going to be at the meeting. It is possible that actual attendance is poor when compared to potential attendance because the chapter houses are located too far away from hogans. These and other causes have been stated by Navajo informants as reasons for not attending chapter meetings. However, many informants said that they did not need to attend the chapter meetings in order to know what went on, for usually one or more of their extended family members attended and upon their return recounted the chapter activities to the absent members. In addition according to my observations, a high proportion of those people

TABLE 2.—*Membership and average attendance in 40 Navajo chapter meetings* [1]

Chapter House	Estimated Chapter Membership	Estimated Average Attendance
Alamo, N. Mex	400	60
Baca, N. Mex	650	30
Bird Spring, Ariz	375	100
Canyoncito, N. Mex	300	75
Casamero Lake, N. Mex	441	75
Chilchinbito, Ariz	1, 068	50
Chinle, Ariz	900	75
Coal Mine Mesa, Ariz	280	100
Dalton Pass, N. Mex	250	60
Dilcon, Ariz	600	90
Hard Rock, Ariz	420	103
Huerfano, N. Mex	500	75
Indian Wells, Ariz	320	60
Iyanbito, N. Mex	425	55
Klagetoh, Ariz	450	150
Lake Valley, N. Mex	489	60
Lupton, Ariz	700	60
Manuelito, N. Mex	1, 225	60
Many Farms, Ariz	1, 200	125
Mariana Lake, N. Mex	1, 600	60
Mexican Springs, N. Mex	850	100
Nageezi, N. Mex	800	65
Naschitti, N. Mex	1, 100	80
Navajo Mountain, Utah	400	65
Nazlini, Ariz	500	80
Oak Springs, Ariz	300	30
Pinedale, N. Mex	904	50
Piñon, Ariz	1, 000	120
Red Lake, Ariz.[2]	300	65
Red Rock, N. Mex	750	90
Rock Point, Ariz	550	130
Rock Springs, N. Mex	330	65
Round Rock, Ariz	650	105
St. Michaels, Ariz	1, 165	75
Sanasti, N. Mex	950	60
Sawmill, Ariz	1, 058	85
Smith Lake, N. Mex	800	98
Teec Nos Pos, N. Mex	850	75
Teastoh, Ariz	1, 500	60
Twin Lakes, N. Mex	1, 050	50
Total	28, 400	3, 071
Average	710	77

[1] Figures obtained from officers of these chapters during interviews in 1962.

[2] In grazing district no. 18.

attending chapter meetings were older, less likely to be able to speak English, and less likely to be able to qualify for full-time employment on or off the Navajo Reservation. The correspondence between the 11 percent derived from the figures given in Table 2, and the 12.3 percent 1960 census figure for the segment of Navajo population 45 years and older (Young, 1961, p. 328) is striking, especially in view of my observation that older Navajos constitute the majority of people who attend chapter meetings regularly.

It is my belief that the low attendance at meetings is not an indication of a lack of interest in chapter affairs or its organization. Chapter meetings are well attended at election dates, during discussions concerning the use of a chapter house by a missionary for Sunday services, during discussions concerning the trader in the community, or during the time a chapter serves as a "court of domestic relations." Attendance at chapter meetings is high when decisions are to be made regarding community projects, and who is to be selected to work on those "relief" projects which are financially underwritten by the Navajo Tribe.

The usual number of meetings a chapter holds during a month's time is three (Tables 3, 4, and 5) and it is possible that meetings are held too frequently for the average membership. The fact that chapter officers can hold three meetings a month for which they receive a per diem allowance of $17 for each meeting, very likely prevents most chapter officers from holding fewer meetings to suit their respective memberships. However, many chapters do not hold all of the 36 meetings allowed them annually under tribal regulations.

In each of the 65 chapter communities surveyed in 1962, there was a strong and active interest in chapter affairs, as measured by the intensity with which the members discussed issues, especially among the people judged to be 30 years of age or older. Navajos who were middle-age or older (45 years) were observed to occupy the positions of president and vice-president of the chapter, and very frequently a younger person served the chapter as the secretary. About one-third of the secretaries were women but only three women had been elected to the position of president of a chapter. In general, Navajo women are accorded less respect than men when they rise and speak during a chapter meeting; however, the points they make concerning an issue are often incorporated into a man's talk later and used as a basis of chapter action.[17]

The data in Tables 3, 4, and 5, for the activities of the chapters at Casamero Lake, Chinle, and Navajo Mountain have been divided into four main categories. The first main section is devoted to the presentation of reports to the chapter from political units among the Navajo which encompass more people and a greater geographical area than the individual chapters. Chapters throughout Navajo country receive reports from Council

[17] Few Navajo women have been elected to political offices within the Navajo governmental structure. However, many serve as administrative assistants and secretaries; e.g., Katherine Arviso was recently appointed administrative assistant to Raymond Nakai, Chairman of the Navajo Tribe. Katherine Arviso is the daughter of Jake Watchman, a highly respected leader from the Crystal area of the reservation, and is a graduate of the University of Arizona.

TABLE 3.—*Casamero Lake Chapter meetings: 1960–61*

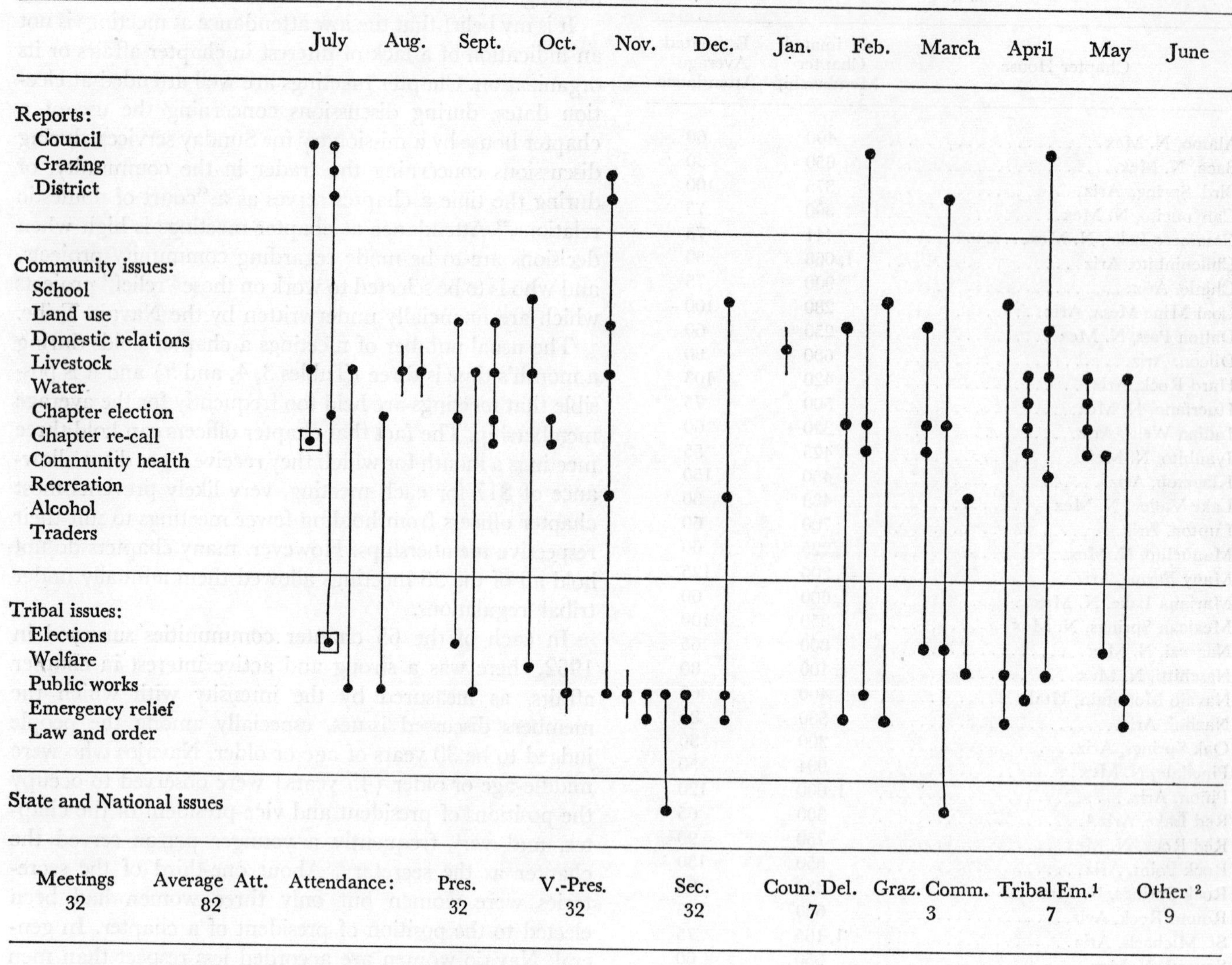

Key: Discussion ☐Vote on issue Single meeting

[1] Tribal Em. includes: Community workers, tribal laywers, etc.
[2] Other includes: B.I.A., U.S.P.H.S., State employees, missionaries, traders and tourists.

delegates on the proceedings of the Navajo Tribal Council. Council reports to chapters are not scheduled; however, the usual time of the report to a chapter is during or just after a Council session, of which there are four a year. The attendance of Council delegates at chapter meetings is not mandatory; the frequency of their attendance plus the number of reports given during a year's time, can serve as a rough measure of a Council delegate's interest in chapter activities. In these terms, the Council delegate elected from the Navajo Mountain area rates the highest of the three chapters.

The reports from the district grazing committee are also listed, as are their attendance records. Frequently, chapters suspend their own meeting for a short period (two or three hours) while the grazing committee conducts a meeting for the benefit of the assembled group. At other times, a member of the grazing committee will give a report to a chapter, informing them of new regulations, rules, and problems. The third kind of report is that from the district tribal council. This political unit is composed of all Council delegates, chapter officers, and grazing committee members who are elected to serve the Navajos within the land management district.

The district tribal council attempts to coordinate district-wide projects and programs, such as ram herds, rodent control, spring development, soil erosion, and livestock improvement, and it meets as a body about every 6 weeks. The district tribal council is an outgrowth of meetings held, during the 1930's and 1940's, by the supervisor of the land management district to which Council delegates and rangeriders were invited and asked to discuss and formulate programs for the entire land manage-

TABLE 4.—*Chinle Chapter meetings: 1960–61*

	July	Aug.	Sept.	Oct.	Nov.	Dec.	Jan.	Feb.	March	April	May	June
Reports:												
Council												
Grazing												
District												
Community issues:												
School												
Land use												
Domestic relations												
Livestock												
Water												
Chapter elections												
Chapter re-call												
Community health												
Recreation												
Alcohol												
Traders												
Tribal issues:												
Elections												
Welfare												
Public works												
Emergency relief												
Law and order												
State and National issues												

Meetings	Average Att.	Attendance:	Pres.	V.-Pres.	Sec.	Coun. Del.	Graz. Comm.	Tribal Em.[1]	Other[2]
33	82		26	23	24	5	14	19	27

Key: Discussion Vote on issue Single meeting

[1] Tribal Em. includes: Community workers, tribal lawyers, etc.

[2] Other includes: B.I.A., U.S.P.H.S., State employees, missionaries, traders and tourists.

ment district. In recent years, most grazing districts have reinstituted the district-wide meeting, and elected a chairman and vice-chairman to guide the meetings. To date, the district tribal council has not been successful in formulating programs for the people within the various districts. This is due in part to its nebulous power and lack of organization, and in part to the fact that in many cases chapter areas cut across district lines (map 1). Normally one or more local chapter officers attend the district tribal council meetings and report to their groups what was discussed.

The second major category of chapter activities is given under Community Issues. The list of items is not exhaustive, for I observed that such delicate items of discussion as witchcraft being practiced among several members of a chapter were not reported in the minutes recorded by a chapter secretary. However, the list of topics is typical of all 96 chapters in Navajo country, as is the frequency of discussion of topics.

It is to be noted that in a meeting discussing livestock or water, there frequently is a corresponding discussion item marked under Emergency Relief or Public Works. Thus the line drawn between Community Issues and Tribal Issues is used to facilitate the reading of Tables 3–5 and does not represent real patterns of discussion among Navajos. The real pattern of discussion among chapter members begins with, for example, an announcement from the chapter president that the Navajo Tribe has allotted a sum of money to the chapter for public works projects, and usually the president would give the details of how the chapter could use the money. This discussion would be listed under Tribal Issues along the topic line of Public Works.

In the event the meeting then moved into a discussion

TABLE 5.—*Navajo Mountain Chapter meetings: 1960–61*

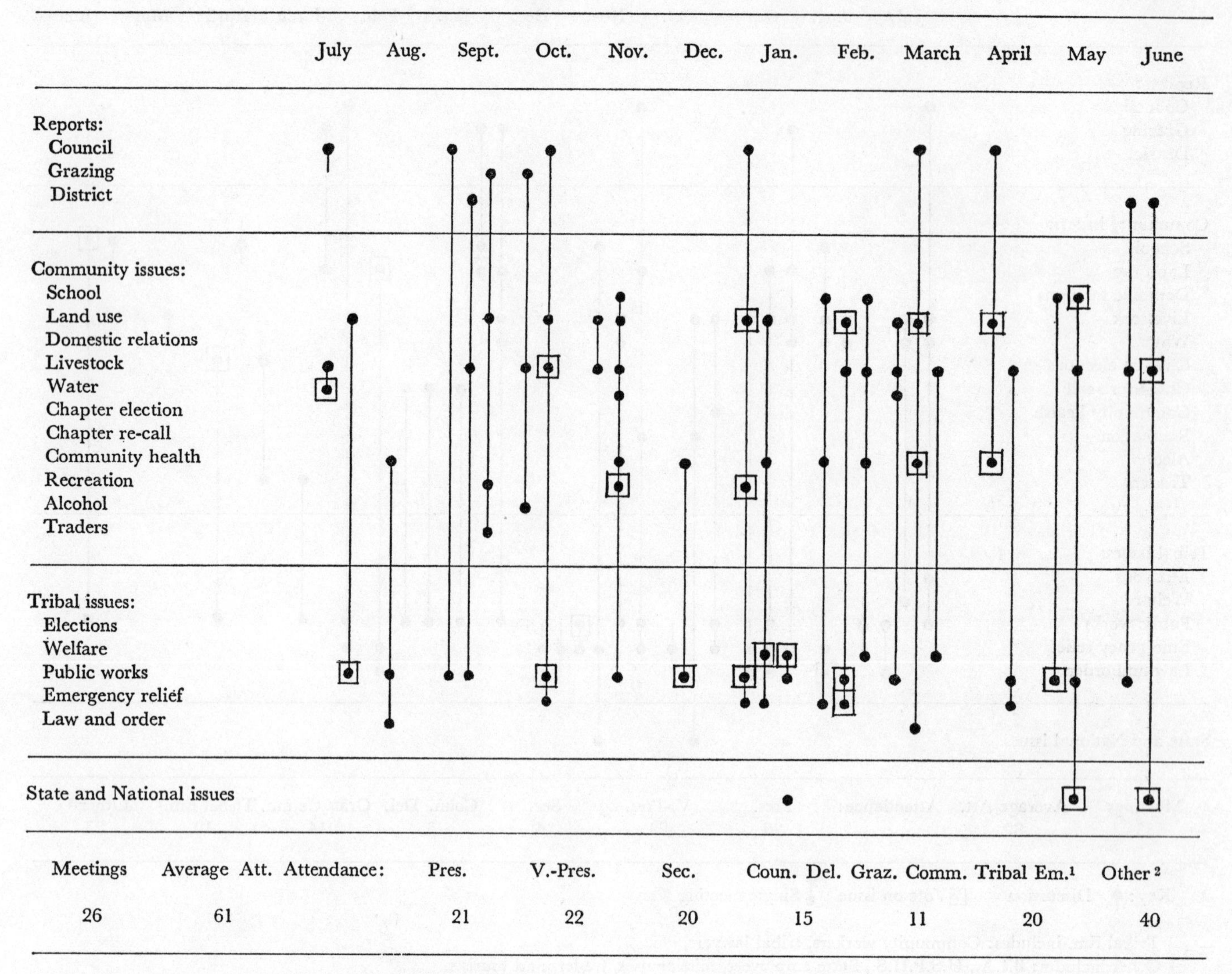

[1] Tribal Em. includes: Community workers, tribal laywers, etc.
[2] Other includes: B.I.A., U.S.P.H.S., State employees, missionaries, traders and tourists.

of what they as a chapter might do in the way of a community improvement project under the guidelines of the public works program, the discussion would be listed under various items in the Community Issues column. In like manner, a Council report often prompts a discussion on Emergency Relief or Law and Order, or a grazing report starts a discussion on land use and livestock.

The infrequency of some items of discussion may indicate that the membership did not consider these areas particularly in need of adjustment; that these items were discussed outside of the chapter; or that the subject matter was not considered appropriate in a written report. I observed that discussions concerning bootlegging, peyote, witchcraft, stealing, adultery, ceremonials, wife beating, and funerals seldom were a part of chapter activities. Occasionally however, a chapter meeting discussed a particular family's domestic relations, and in one case a chapter membership was requested to vote on whether or not the chapter house could be used as a place in which funeral services might be held for a departed member (the request was voted down).

The fourth major category is State and National Issues. Under this heading are placed discussions such as occurred in the Navajo Mountain Chapter, e.g., relinguishment of reservation land to the Federal Government for the establishment of a National Park at Rainbow Bridge or, as in the case of Chinle, the restoration of Canyon De Chelly, a National Park, to the Navajo Tribe. The chapter discussions of State issues were concerned almost exclusively with State welfare benefits and the rights of Navajos to vote in State elections.

The most distinguishing feature of the activities of the three chapters is the difference in the frequency of voting on a motion. Navajo Mountain Chapter voted on motions 24 times during a year of activity, whereas Chinle Chapter voted 7 times, and Casamero Lake Chapter voted only twice during the same period. It was inferred earlier that voting in chapters was a symbolic means by which a chapter expressed community solidarity, rather than being exclusively a means to activate a program. The data from the three chapters supports this inference. An examination of the minutes from each of the three chapters reveals considerable disharmony within the Casamero Lake Chapter, a moderate amount of disharmony in the Chinle Chapter, and a high degree of community solidarity in the Navajo Mountain Chapter.

The Casamero Lake Chapter began the year's activity with a vote to recall the chapter president; while this motion was passed by the membership, they were never able to bring about a change in who was to occupy the chapter president's chair. It is to be noted that the issue of chapter elections was discussed in 11 of the 22 meetings, and the issue of recall was discussed in 7 meetings, yet neither issue reached a vote other than at the first meeting. The basic problem at Casamero Lake was the accusation that the president consistently placed his relatives in the groups of workers doing community improvement projects, for which the Navajo Tribe paid each worker $1.25 an hour. The Navajo Tribe had allotted various sums of money for public works projects and emergency relief programs to each community or chapter. The chapter officers in each area were to assign jobs to the neediest people in their respective communities, and no person was to have a job on one of the "relief" projects for more than two weeks. However, the president of the Casamero Lake Chapter was accused of not spreading out the jobs among all the members of the community, but instead putting his male and female relatives on the "relief roll" week after week.

In contrast, the Navajo Mountain Chapter handled this work project issue smoothly, with the chapter membership voting frequently on how the tribal money was to be used, and what community project was of greatest benefit to the people. A clue to the reason why there was less outward friction at Navajo Mountain in these matters is provided by comparing the clan affiliation and numerical rank of the officers in each chapter organization as given in Table 6. The first two chapter officers and the council delegate of Navajo Mountain belong to the clan in the area with the greatest numerical strength. This is not the case with either the Casamero Lake or Chinle chapters, where the elective offices of the chapters are held by individuals of the lower numerical ranking clans. In addition, the

TABLE 6.—*Clan affiliation of elected local leaders*

Clans	Members [1]	Rank	Pres.	Vice Pres.	Sec.	Coun. Mem.
Casamero Lake:						
Kiiya'aani	350	1				
Tsi'naajinii	300	2	X			
Yoo'o	175	3		X		
Haaltso	35	4			X	X
Tohbaazhna'azh	20	5				
Todokonzh	15	6				
Tabaha	10	7				
Total	805					
Chinle:						
Kiiya'aani	600	1				X
To'hed Łiini	450	2				
Todich'iini	250	3				
Ma'ideshghiisnii	200	4	X			
Tabaha	200	5		X		
Tsi'naajinii	50	6				
Hoonagahni	40	7				
Totsooni	40	8			X	
Tłaaschii'	40	9				
Dibe Tlizhiini	25	10				
Taachnii'nii	15	11				
Total	2, 010					
Navajo Mountain:						
Ashiihi	400	1	X	X		X
Todich'iini	200	2				
Kiiya'aani	50	3			X	
Bit'ahnii	50	4				
Tabaanhi	50	5				
Taachii'nii	50	6				
Tłiziłani	30	7				
Lok'aadine'e	20	8				
Total	850					

[1] Estimates provided by officers and members of each chapter.

Chinle data indicate that the leaders of the most populous clan have withdrawn from active participation within the Chinle Chapter and have attempted to promote its political interest by electing a delegate to the Navajo Tribal Council.

The Chinle Chapter membership voted to recall all of its officers; even though the petition was withdrawn in a succeeding meeting, the president resigned and a new man was elected to his position. The chapter officers of Chinle were accused of improper leadership and, in particular, allowing social dances to be held at the chapter house. One of the chapter officers responded to the criticism by stating that "nothing goes on at the chapter hops that does not occur at Yeibichai and Squaw Dances, and here we have electric lights."

The topics that received the most attention of the three chapters presented in Tables 3–5 are typical of all 96 chapters in Navajo country.[18] There is considerable discussion and some voting on livestock, water, and land-use matters. There is also considerable interest in what goods and services can be provided for them by outside agencies, such as the Navajo Tribe, State welfare and employment bureaus, the Bureau of Indian Affairs, and the U.S. Public Health Service. The Navajos making up the memberships of the 96 chapters in Navajo country are not passive recipients of the ideas and services offered them, but take an active part in deciding in their chapter meetings what is acceptable and what should be rejected or "tabled" for the present time.

[18] The official chapter minutes for each of the 96 units for the period from July 1, 1960, to June 20, 1961, were analyzed by me.

Navajo Political Behavior

The apparent ease with which most contemporary Navajos use Anglo-American political principles in the operation of their self-government units can mislead one who seeks an understanding of the conceptions Navajos have of their political organizations, especially if one were to accept the terminology used in Navajo political meetings as indicative of cultural content. It was pointed out earlier that all of the current self-government organizations among the Navajo on the community, regional, and tribal level were introduced and sponsored by Government agencies in an attempt to modify the Navajo cultural system. As the Navajo adjusted to the new forms of political organization derived from Indo-European cultural models, they began to incorporate such political principles as majority rule, quorum, standing vote, and parliamentary procedures such as tabling a motion. However, the meaning each of these political features has for Anglo-Americans is different from the meaning it has for the Navajo.

One of the outstanding differences in the cultural content or the meaning a political action has for Americans as opposed to Navajos is the sentiment each attaches to an active aggressive minority bloc of voters in a political meeting. Generally, the Americans view the minority group in a political meeting with satisfaction and consider its presence a measure of a vigorous and healthy state of political affairs. The presence of an active minority bloc of voters in a Navajo political meeting is viewed with considerable dissatisfaction and is thought to represent an unhealthy state of political affairs. The problems caused by a minority were discussed earlier in reference to the Twin Lakes Chapter. A similar "minority" problem occurred at the Becenti Chapter meeting held on September 16, 1961. The Becenti chapter house is located about 12 miles north of Crownpoint, N. Mex., on a dirt road. There are no other buildings (trading posts, hogans, framehouses, schools, or clinics) within a 2-mile radius of the Becenti chapter house which was built by community labor in 1935. The issue facing the chapter membership at Becenti was whether or not to put the sum of money ($4,500) allotted the chapter by the Navajo Tribe for public works projects in a bank or start community projects immediately. As it turned out, a large majority of the members present at the meeting voted to put the money in a commercial bank located in Gallup, New Mexico. A minority of three women and one man opposed this action, however, for they wanted to begin several community projects right away. This political action took 6 hours to complete. One of the women who opposed the majority said:

> My president, Council delegate and visitors, I am going to cover a few things that have been accomplished in the past by the use of public works projects in our community. We have had road work for our people; we have had school shelters built for our children so they don't have to stand in the rain and cold weather. Our leaders in Window Rock have given us some money now to do more for our people living now, and I think we need to follow this lead and build some hogans for older people that have no good place to live in. Our leaders in Window Rock did not tell us to put this money away for a rainy day; I say it is already raining on us.

[The concluding statement evidently amused most of the membership for there were many smiles and some members whispered comments to those close by. The next speaker recognized by the chapter president was the Council delegate from the Becenti area who said:]

> I support the suggestions by [woman's name] that the money be used to help the needy people in this community. The council has sent to each community some money and it is to be used in the way everyone thinks it ought to be used. I think that most of you people don't

321-627—70——5

agree with me, but this woman and others need to have some to build a hogan to live in, and that is what the council acted out this public works resolution for. All we want to know is how the money is going to be used, and this woman has a project in mind.

[The next speaker was an older man who sat at the front of the meeting and next to the Council delegate. This elder said:]

Mr. Chairman, vice-chairman, secretary, Council delegate, visitors and chapter members, I have lived a long time. I have lived before there was a council to hand out money. I think money is not like a relative when you need help, for money is what is troubling us here today. We need to think of it as a long term thing. There is no end to money; it comes to you and it goes away and comes again. It is not like sheep but cold. We have to think hard on this money for it is pumped out of the ground.

We are told that soon there will be work here when our new chapter house gets started. I helped build this chapter house, but we did not get money for that, only a little corn for our horses from Washington. There will be money for those people who get work on this new chapter house project, and that is the way we should be looking. If the woman back there wants to have money, let her work on the chapter house and we can save the other for after that.

The president and secretary of the chapter spoke after the elder had finished and agreed with his position. In addition, many other chapter members spoke in favor of saving the public works money for a time when there was a greater need for wagework. The minority position was restated several times by the woman who had first voiced her objections to putting the money in the bank.

Three hours after the discussion had started, a motion was made to put the public works money in a bank and the motion was quickly seconded. However, the discussion continued for about 2½ hours more, at which time the community worker assigned to this chapter as a tribal employee suggested that the issue be brought to a vote. Following this suggestion three people rose and spoke in favor of bringing the issue to a vote, and the president called for a standing vote of all those who favored putting the public works money in the bank. Thirty-six chapter members stood up and four remained seated, whereupon the chapter president asked the three visitors (a community worker, a Navajo tribal policeman and the writer) to make a count of those standing. When the count was given to the president, he asked that all chapter members who were in favor of putting the public works money in the bank to stand again so that everyone could be counted. The count was repeated and the four members who had remained seated on the first count remained seated on the second. The chapter president then asked all those who did not favor putting the money in the bank to stand, and three women and one man raised their right hands. The chapter secretary reported to the chapter that the motion had passed with 36 votes in favor and 4 opposed. At this moment the three women who had raised their hands in opposition to the motion got up and walked hurriedly toward the door of the meeting room, but before they reached the door the Council delegate began speaking and said:

Wait! You women wait! I want to speak before you leave. There are things here that are not settled. The Navajo people always help each other and do not turn away from those who are Navajos, that is not the Navajo way. This is no time to leave with angry thoughts; there is money here for those that need it, and I suggest that if anybody here needs $5 or $10 or whatever for food, clothing, or something they can get it from the president or the secretary as a loan. The money for the loan can be taken out of the public works money and there will only be a small interest in the bank for it will be in a checking account. I will see to it personally that this will be done, and I say, let's all stand and say to each other that this is what will be done the way I have outlined it.

[Many people were already standing when the Council delegate spoke, for they were preparing to leave, and the rest stood up as the suggestion was made. The Becenti Chapter meeting concluded as the president said:]

This is what I have to say. I agree that the money is to be in the bank, and I told you that this is what we had to do when the meeting started, therefore I will close the meeting now.

The drama prompted by the Council delegate's last minute suggestion that the members of the chapter stand up as a body to signify unanimous concern over the plight of the three women who needed money tends to overshadow the two other major attempts at gaining a consensus on the issue faced by the Becenti Chapter. Throughout the meeting those who talked tried to make the minority change their opinion and join the majority. The double vote count is interpreted as a move by the chapter president to allow the minority to change their minds after seeing the strength of their numbers. When these two techniques failed to sway the minority however, the Council delegate chose a propitious moment to suggest that everyone stand up to gain a consensus, for many individuals were already on their feet preparing to leave the meeting hall. Thus the meeting disbanded at least upon a note of harmony and unanimity.

The Council delegate explained his action after the meeting as one which would "allow those women and that man to come to future chapter meetings, for everyone agreed that they were in need of financial assistance." The delegate also suggested that "unless something had been done they would have blamed me and the rest of the people for their troubles." On the basis of these statements it is inferred that all of the chapter members who were in attendance that day at Becenti felt a sense of relief for having the meeting end upon a note of harmony and with a sense of common concern with the women who were making a hasty exit.

The wisdom of the Council delegate in choosing just the right medium through which the members were able to express their sentiments toward consensus should not be overlooked. The delegate interrelated the minority opinion on money matters with the majority sentiment toward harmony, and it is inferred that he wished to have a public acknowledgment of the financial crises faced by the three women. Conceptually, a private misfortune was made public at the Becenti Chapter meeting and, while the majority of members at this meeting refused to accept the solution offered by the minority, the entire group responded to the suggestion offered by the Council delegate to express their sense of moral responsibility for one of their neighbors, thus ending the meeting on a note of harmony.

The strong emotions attached to those people who adopt a minority position at a Navajo political gathering was also illustrated at a chapter meeting held at Oak Springs in 1961. The Oak Springs Chapter area is located about 10 miles south of Fort Defiance, Ariz. In recent years the Oak Springs Chapter membership has been politically divided over the proposed location of a new chapter house. A minority faction in the general Oak Springs Chapter membership wanted two smaller meeting houses to be constructed in two different locations, so that meetings could be held alternately in each locality. A compromise was worked out which allowed the numerically smaller group at Pine Springs to have a smaller meeting place erected in their area, with the main chapter house to be built at Oak Springs which was centrally located for the majority of the members of the chapter. However, several residents of the Pine Springs area continued to voice their opinion that the compromise was unacceptable because the meeting halls were of different size and the Pine Springs chapter house would lack such items as modern gas stoves, folding chairs, tables, and a butane heating system.

The Pine Springs group of dissenters wanted each area to have equal accommodations or none at all for either area, and to promote this point of view an older well-known Navajo man from the Pine Springs area was allowed to make the opening statement at the chapter meeting held at Oak Springs on May 21, 1961. This elder said:

> I have here with me a typewritten petition which I made for you people to discuss concerning the funds for the public works. The petition is for the setting up of a community house at Pine Springs and an equal size community house at Oak Springs here.
>
> My plan is to use the money allotted us for building a new chapter house at Oak Springs to build two community houses of equal size in both places, and if this cannot be done then let us use public works money for this thing.

[The next speaker was an elder from the Oak Springs area who said:]

> Mr. Chairman and you people who are attending. I want to come straight to the point of what I have to say. I think [man's name] petition is not favorable as the Pine Springs' community house issue has been discussed several times and the people decided to go ahead and build the Pine Springs' people a community house and to build the new chapter house here at Oak Springs.

[The third man to speak at the meeting was the chapter president who said:]

> I also want to express my opinion against the petition that has been presented by [man's name] at this time. I believe that we chapter officers should be the ones to plan the agenda for the meetings and if we want a petition, let the people decide and discuss it before a petition is presented. As of now we don't know what and who planned this petition, all except for [man's name], so I think it is better to discuss these with the people instead of writing the petition without the people knowing anything about it.

[At this point the petitioner jumped to his feet and as he held the petition so all could see it said:]

> Are you accusing me of writing a petition without the people knowing it? I've talked to the Council members about it and they advised me to write a petition. Therefore if you people don't want this petition I will dispose of it. I'm leaving now!

As the resident from Pine Springs finished this statement he crumpled his petition and thrust it into his pants' pocket and rapidly walked out of the meeting hall. No one at the meeting followed him from the hall, and soon the chapter meeting began to discuss local issues such as sheep dipping, pasturage for the ram herd, and the need to repair the wooden bridges in the area. The only mention of the hasty exit of the elder from Pine Springs was made toward the end of the meeting by a visitor from another area who was a member of the grazing committee for the district. This man said: "I think the petition presented at the beginning of this meeting was for the use of

Government funds not for tribal funds and we should have listened to what he had to say instead of running him off. His idea was to get information on this subject; not to tell you people what to do." There was no response to the visitor's statement, and the meeting ended with no further discussion on the location of the chapter house.

There is great similarity in the actions by the petitioner from Pine Springs and the three women of Becenti who attempted to leave their chapter meeting when they were forced to reveal their minority opinion on an issue. In both cases the behavior of the individuals was to withdraw from the group which did not share their point of view. The same reaction was noted earlier in the behavior of Jacob Morgan as he walked out of the 1937 Constitutional Assembly after denouncing a proposal on the floor that a committee be set up to write a constitution for the Navajo. There are strong indications that Jacob Morgan was following a pattern of behavior that has long existed in Navajo culture, for there is Old Nata's account of the "last *naachid*" in which the peace chief Nataleeth withdrew from the "council" subsequent to its decision to go to war against the Americans in 1857. Even earlier, there was the mass withdrawal of the Cebolleta Navajos from under the protective supervision of the Franciscan Friars in 1750. Thus there is a long record of individuals and groups withdrawing from sociopolitical situations at crucial points of decision among the Navajos. These instances of withdrawal indicate a major culture pattern among the Navajos, yet they are descriptive of an extreme action which is undertaken only after efforts at compromise have failed. Logically, there ought to be alternative means to achieve withdrawal that would not cause as much disharmony.

My participant observation at over 100 sociopolitical gatherings among contemporary Navajos revealed three means of withdrawing from a gathering that caused little or no discord among the members of the groups. The first is obviously nonattendance at a meeting. This action presupposes knowledge about what will be discussed; and as agendas of chapter, grazing, and council meetings are made public before the date of the meeting, nonattendance because of disagreements is possible. Also, most meetings of a political nature are extremely slow to start, and information as to what will be discussed is available by word of mouth to those who might be interested. Thus, a person can come to a meeting early and learn enough about the main topics and attitudes toward the topics before the actual meeting starts, and absent himself if his opinion is not of the majority.

Closely related to nonattendance as an alternative pattern of withdrawal is behavior best described as "doorway" withdrawal. This involves an individual standing at the door of the meeting hall where he can hear the discussion sufficiently well, and can move either to the outside of the meeting place or inside to make a point or vote if he so desires. At most chapter and grazing committee meetings one can observe clusters of men and women standing in the one or more doorways to the hall, even though there are available empty seats in the meeting hall. These clusters will reduce in size during vote counting and passage in and out of the meeting hall is easiest during voting. During the colder winter months the doorways to inside rooms such as to the storerooms or kitchen of chapter houses are utilized by the "doorway" groups as strategic positions from which to withdraw or enter into the activities of the group.

Statements from the individuals who stand in doorways at Navajo political meetings vary from noncommittal answers such as, "It is too stuffy in there—I can't get my breath," to defensive answers such as, "I know what is going to be said—I don't need to be inside, as there are people there who will vote my way anyway," or "They're talking crazy in there. Something got into them, and they don't know what they are doing—I'll go back later but not now." When such "doorway" informants were questioned about whether or not they would take a seat when they returned to the meeting the answer was invariably *datsi,* which means "maybe" in Navajo.

The third means of achieving a withdrawal is directly related to political action, and is the utilization of the motion to "table" an issue and thereby relieve the participants from public demonstration of disharmony. Frequently the actual motion for tabling is not made, seconded, and voted upon, but instead the president of a chapter merely states: "We seem divided on this issue, therefore I put it on the table until we all think more alike on it" (Crystal Chapter notes, May 12, 1962) or, "There are not enough important people here today to work on this thing, and I think we need them to help us think on this issue, therefore we will take it up later" (Alamo Chapter notes, November 21, 1961). One result of tabling a motion is to allow the people to think, discuss, and form opinions on an issue at their leisure. These discussions are carried on at the trading post, in the hogans, at squaw dances and other ceremonials, as well as at schools, missions, and BIA and tribal offices.

Often, a chapter will ask an "expert" to come to their meeting to inform them on a subject. During my stay with the Navajo the issue of electrical powerlines crossing the reservation was discussed in many chapters. Each chapter had the right to approve or disapprove the passage of the powerlines over its area, and thus the topic occupied many chapter agendas for many months. The power companies got tribal approval but needed local approval before constructing their towers and putting in lines. The most frequent question asked by the local groups was whether or not the powerlines would affect their sheep, and many experts were faced with answering this question. Many Navajos felt uneasy about the answers given to this question. One Navajo man said:

> The power men want to use our land to carry their electricity, but when they use our land for this purpose, we Navajos ought to be told just what electricity is, and I have asked a dozen of those men, and none of them can explain what it is. I say, that until they can tell us what electricity is, we don't want it over our heads and over our sheep. We have to know how to protect ourselves and sheep in the case something goes wrong.

In most chapters the powerline issue was tabled and discussions were carried on outside of the local chapters; the erection of powerlines across the Navajo Reservation was delayed 6 to 8 months. The first chapter to approve the passage of the powerlines across its area was Kin Li Chee. This chapter held meetings for several months on the issue, and called in "experts" to advise them. The outstanding figure in the political process was the Council delegate from the Kin Li Chee area. After the chapter had voted approval this man said:

> There were many people opposed to this project of powerlines through the Kin Li Chee area, but they were afraid of what this thing was going to do to the area. Navajos like to have time to think about something as new as electricity over their land. I had voted for the proposal in the Council and therefore it was my duty to tell the people that elected me what this project was all about.
>
> I see the people of Kin Li Chee many time a week, and as there was an archeological site in the area being made into a Tribal Park, I was there at all of the chapter meetings getting them to approve the withdrawal of that land. The new Tribal Park would bring strangers onto the area, and many people objected to that, but it might also bring in some money, therefore most of the people felt this project was a good idea. Next came the powerlines.
>
> I spoke to the chapter many times. I had some of the engineers come and talk to the Kin Li Chee Chapter. The younger people felt good about the powerlines for it would give them some wagework near their homes, but the older people thought about it differently. They thought all around the subject, and wanted to know how this new thing would affect their life. There was no way to explain how much good it would do them, for none of the electricity was to be used for their hogans . . . so I made the point that it was not going to help them or harm them. I guess the main objection was whether or not the powerlines would bring more lightning . . . and I said I didn't know about that, but the power people said it would not bring any more. I don't think the people believed the power people on the lightning thing, and I don't know about it myself.
>
> The thing that finally decided the question was that the elders of the community saw that they were not giving up any land to outsiders, and that any time the Tribe wanted to, it could tell these people to take down the powerlines.

It is evident that the Council delegate had to convince the elders of the Kin Li Chee Chapter area before a consensus on the powerline issue could be resolved. The most influential members of a chapter were identified earlier as the "inner council of leaders" and are thought to represent the core of the decisionmaking group of each chapter. It was to these men that the Council delegate looked for support and understanding. According to his statement, he got their approval and, in turn, the members of the chapter voted in favor of the erection of steel towers with high voltage electrical lines through the Kin Li Chee area. Consensus was achieved in Kin Li Chee on the powerline issue, and they point with pride to the fact that not only had they built one of the first chapter houses in Navajo country, but that they were the first community to have the powerlines built through their area. The pride mentioned above as a characteristic attitude among the membership of the Kin Li Chee Chapter membership, however, is to be interpreted as an aspect of a general feeling of harmony and well-being within the community.

The detailed history of the decision to permit the electric powerlines to cross the Kin Li Chee area was given by the chapter president (Interview, March 14, 1962):

> Yes, we were very undecided about this thing, and I was also worried about it, for it was new to us, and while we have had such things as schools, paved roads, and a chapter organization for a long time, this power company project was new. After a while we got the suggestion that those people who have grazing land and hogans nearest the powerlines be the ones to talk the most. It was felt that these people had more to say about it than the rest of us who live miles from the lines.
>
> These people were the ones who decided that it was not going to hurt them very much by having the towers on their land, and the rest agree that was the thing to do. We also agree that these people who lived nearest the powerlines should be the first people employed, just as we tried to do at the Tribal Park's project.

[The chapter president also stated that there were objections from other people in the Kin Li Chee area over the location of the powerlines because]

> . . . they had children in school and the school was near the powerline path. Some other people said it [the powerline] was in a bad place because it was passing

close to the chapter house, and they had to go under it to get to a meeting. We did not hear much from these people later when it was said that those living nearest the lines should do the talking . . . they didn't like it, but when we voted it in I only saw a few of them standing against it.

The means by which harmony and consensus was achieved by the Kin Li Chee Chapter in regard to the powerline issue reveal the intimate functional relationship between consensus and the behavior pattern I have called withdrawal. I believe that the interdependent functions of withdrawal and consensus characterize most, if not all, contemporary Navajo sociopolitical structures.

A major emphasis of all Navajo social interaction is to achieve harmony, and the well-being of individuals is coextensive with that of the group (Albert, 1956, p. 233). Harmonious interpersonal relations are thus the primary objective of action, and consensus is the direct evidence that a group has reached its goal. Consensus among the Navajos is not so much an agreement on all issues as it is the pattern of discussion, debate, negotiation, and compromise, and the respect for attitudes of indifference among members of its group whose primary aim is to maintain a sense of identification with each other as participants in the Navajo culture. The act of withdrawing from a social or political gathering by individuals is behavior prompted by considerable social pressure for consensus and harmony which, in turn, is valued by Navajos as the greatest good in the universe (Ibid.).

Utilizing our postulate that the achievement of consensus or near consensus functions to maintain a sense of cultural identification with fellow Navajos as they participate in various sociopolitical structures, the assumption is made that the activities of a chapter provide a means by which Navajos can realize a sense of identification on the local land-use community level. The same assumption can be made for those people among the Navajos generally who have retained the traditional transhumant livestock pattern of subsistence as they deal with grazing and livestock matters in the operation of the district grazing committees. The Navajo Tribal Council provides a means by which all Navajos can maintain a sense of identification as Navajos whether or not they live on or off of the reservation.

Political Incorporation

The development of several contemporary political structures among the Navajo has been discussed in the preceding chapters and can now be summarized. To accomplish this, it will be necessary to restate the conditions under which contact took place between Navajos and Whites and to discuss the integration of cultural elements that took place as a result of contact. In terms of the present study, the most outstanding feature of the integrative process undergone by the Navajo has been a major trend toward structural incorporation of Anglo-American principles of political organization without a corresponding strong tendency to integrate the cultural content of these principles.

Structural incorporation is operationally defined here as the integration of a network of selected social statuses derived from one social system with statuses of another system; it differs from the integration of cultural content which refers to the adjustment of beliefs, attitudes, and sentiments to form a single system (Eggan, 1950, p. 6). A clear example of structural incorporation was given earlier (see p. 35 above) by Howard Gorman, who related that when a chapter was established at Ganado ". . . we called our leader President instead of *sha hastoui* (my elder), but we meant the same thing." Another example was provided by John Perry's description (see pp. 33–34) of S. F. Stacher's attempt to institute a single Navajo leader for the people living around the Pueblo Bonito school and agency district. Perry's account relates how the Navajo people followed Stacher's instructions and elected a "chief" for all Navajos in the district, but after it was all over ". . . it did not change things very much as we still went to regular leaders and did what they suggested, just as we did before Stacher had the vote . . . ." In both cases the groups of Navajos were linked with Anglo-Americans in a new set of social relations, but the content of the relationships changed little if at all.

The acculturation studies by Dozier (1951 and 1954) of the Hopi-Tewa of Hano strongly indicate that these people have integrated many Hopi social or structural forms while maintaining a distinct cultural individuality during a period of nearly 250 years of close and intimate contact with their hosts, the Hopi of First Mesa. The differential rates for changes in the Hopi-Tewa culture (Dozier, 1954, p. 368)—as a result of the integration of new forms versus new cultural content—tend to corroborate the findings of this present study, thus indicating that changes in cultural forms need not be accomplished by a corresponding shift in cultural content.

The three major political structures (Council, chapter, and grazing committee) introduced and promoted among the Navajo as a part of a directed culture change program of the Government have sufficiently different histories to allow us to compare and evaluate the process of social (form) integration with that of cultural (content) integration. Our attention has been focused on the cultural behavior of Navajos in these three structures, each of which has been considered a "contact center." What is meant by "contact center" is the social relations found to exist among members of the societies in contact at a given time within a given structure. The meaning for "contact center" is identical to that which Spicer has defined as "contact community" (1961, p. 525) except the former is restricted to the structures in which contact takes place. "Contact centers" can be considered the focal points of contact—e.g., trading posts, mission, Tribal Council—between two societies rather than the more general "contact community."

In general, my data suggest that acculturation of the Navajo has proceeded with the least amount of conflict, maladjustment, or disequilibrium when either the form or the content of new cultural elements was principally determined by the Navajo. An obvious corollary of this position is the proposition that when agents of the Anglo-American social system have forced the Navajo to accept both new forms and meanings (as derived from Anglo-American models) there has been considerable cultural disorganization and disequilibrium, which occasionally developed into radical opposition as indicated in conflict between the parties in contact over beliefs, morals, and the roles of the participants.

The theoretical positions taken above have been organized in terms of Vogt's acculturation model of incorporation which he advances as the characteristic integrative process manifest by the Navajo during the last 400 years (Vogt, 1961, p. 328). Incorporation as used by Vogt means the transfer of cultural elements from one culture to another in such a way that these borrowed elements are integrated into the recipient system in terms of its meanings and functions. Vogt's concept of incorporative integration includes the proposition that a condition of cultural stability and equilibirum is maintained. However, recent Navajo culture history indicates considerable disorganization, a fact Vogt seems to be aware of, for he suggests that application of his concept in interpreting this period will require modification of his model. In line with this suggestion, the following refinements are tentatively offered.

One of the strong indications of this study is that the Navajo continued to incorporate new cultural items up to the present time, but accomplished this under special conditions. The Navajo have been subject to a program of directed culture change since they were incarcerated at Fort Sumner in 1864. Ordinarily, incorporative integration does not continue under conditions of directed culture change as it is a process involving a single cultural system's acceptance or rejection of new cultural elements on the basis of its traditional way of life (Spicer, ed., 1961, p. 530). However, incorporative integration ceases as a process only to the extent that the superordinate society's program of culture change is effectively imposed. In the Navajo case, the process was halted at Fort Sumner when the people were forced to accept new cultural elements and their meanings. These conditions continued for the 4-year period they were kept at Fort Sumner and had little or no choice over the form or content of their culture. Upon their release and return to Navajo country in 1868, however, the extent and force of the Government's directed culture change program was greatly relaxed and incorporative integration was renewed.

The Navajo Tribal Council was established by the Government in 1923 as part of the latter's program of directed change. The new political structure was composed of elected Navajos who were to represent the entire Navajo population. The Council was designed to promote more intensive political interaction between Navajos and agents of the Government; replace the Government-appointed Navajo leaders of the tribe with elected representatives; provide the Navajo with a limited degree of political self-determination; and establish a Navajo tribal-wide authority structure which would be responsive to the demands of the Government's program of directed culture change. The history of the Council indicates that for about 10 or 12 years the majority of the Navajo either ignored or were unaware of the existence of the new tribal-wide political structure. On the surface, it appeared that the Navajo had accepted and incorporated into their culture the Navajo Tribal Council. However, subsequent events suggest this point of view was in error.

There is no question but that a number of Navajos did participate in the new political structure, yet the term "incorporate" implies the borrowed elements are fitted into place and conform to the meaningful and functional relations within the borrowing system with little or no disorganization. These conditions obtained insofar as the Navajo culture and the Council were concerned up until 1936 when severe disorganization took place. It was at that time that the Government insisted that the Navajo Tribal Council exercise its tribal authority and approve for the entire Navajo population the Government's program of stock reduction. The Council acted upon the strong, insistent pressure from the Government and passed a resolution giving "tribal" sanction for the program of livestock reduction. The Council attempted to exercise its tribal authority, yet the attempt ended in failure, for the Council did not enjoy any such power at that time. Authority to impose sanctions was still in the hands of chapters or otherwise unorganized outfits. Nevertheless, the Government agents acted as if the Council had such authority and imposed sanctions of its own in a very forceful directed change program. Conflict between the Whites and Navajos developed in structures that linked the two groups; the focal point of conflict concerned the Council, which was dissolved and then reorganized along broader representational lines.

The formation of a new and enlarged Tribal Council composed of 74 elected members did not resolve the conflict between the Navajos and the Indian Agents who were directing the program of culture change. There was serious opposition to the livestock reduction program initiated by the Government for the benefit of the Navajo, and there was opposition in the Council itself over the function of this political structure in regard to its exercise of authority. This is to say, there was a lack of common understanding between Navajos and Whites within the political structure that linked them in a common (yet imperfectly developed) social system. Each respective ethnic group was pursuing different objectives in accordance with two different sets of value orientations.

It appears that the Anglo-Americans guiding the program of stock reduction among Navajos were acting on the assumption that the resources of nature can and should be manipulated for human benefit. Under this scheme of values, land, water, grass, and livestock are to be managed so that men are continually supplied with an abundance of food. Most Navajos opposed this value orientation; they thought of men, land, water, grass, and livestock as interlocked in a system of reciprocity within which an abundance of food was but one manifestation of harmonious interdependence with the forces of nature. High status was accorded those Navajos who exhibited wealth in the form of large herds of livestock (other criteria also were used: ritual knowledge; oratorical ability; knowledge of Navajo myths; and skill in practical affairs such as jewelry making, tanning of hides, lambing, and farming). Thus, for a Navajo to suffer a loss of livestock not only reduced his food supply; it could also cause a loss of prestige. It could be interpreted by members of his group that he had deviated (perhaps unwittingly) from a life of harmony and balance with the rest of nature.

The Government agents insisted that the Tribal Council assist them in setting quotas for various regions in Navajo country. The Council acceded to Government pressure; it helped set prices for stock sold by Navajos, and helped set the number of livestock to be culled from flocks. These actions by elected leaders of the Navajo did not have the support of the general population, for leaders of the people were not expected to make decisions for the group without first obtaining a consensus (or near consensus). Leaders, according to traditional Navajo cultural patterns, are not expected to order other members of their group to behave in a certain manner (certain exceptions occur in ceremonial contexts); on the contrary, leaders are expected to provide members of their group with enough time and information for them to make up their minds about an issue. In terms of traditional Navajo culture, Navajo leaders are expected to participate in ceremonies designed to sanctify major decisions (see pp. 4 ff.) rather than make major decisions for the people.

A result of the conflict over stock reduction, in combination with conflict in regard to the degree of authority exercised by Council members, was that radical opposition developed in the contact centers that linked Navajos and Anglo-Americans during the 1930's and early 1940's. Under such conditions opposition can only be resolved by culture change (Wilson and Wilson, 1945, p. 134). The conflict over the role of leaders could not be solved by replacing leaders because the opposition concerned the cultural content of leadership; either the Anglo-Americans had to accept Navajo ways of leadership or the Navajos had to accept concepts, regarding the role of leaders, held by Anglo-Americans. Radical opposition to Anglo-American concepts of leadership was apparent for many years in the speeches made by Council delegates who insisted on talking at great length about the stock reduction program, instead of talking about matters on the agenda. The Navajo Tribal Council chairman's speech in 1961 to the Central Grazing Committee (see p. 30) is an example of this kind of opposition within the context of the existing political framework. Among the Anglo-Americans, radical opposition was apparent in their constant frustration over the use of "valuable" time by Navajos making long speeches about the stock reduction program (which has passed its peak of intensity) rather than attending to "matters at hand."

In recent years, however, radical opposition has been greatly reduced, although in my opinion it persists among such groups as the grazing committees. Radical opposition has been nearly eliminated in the Tribal Council due to accommodations and adaptations made on both sides. Accommodation among Navajos has come, in part, from a greater awareness of the function of American Government via education in Anglo-American schools, exposure to American ways during military service for the Government, and as a result of contact with Americans in wage-paying jobs away from the Navajo Reservation. In like manner, Americans working with Navajos in these contact centers have learned something of how Navajos maintain social control, the importance Navajos attach to consensus, and how leaders gain and maintain their positions. The Government reduced the intensity of opposition in allowing the Navajo Tribal Council to select its own legal advisor and general counsel in 1947. The objections to a central, tribal-wide political structure with the authority to act on behalf of all Navajos has decreased in recent years as revenue from mineral resources on tribal land (see Table 1, p. 42) has been continually considered an economic asset which belongs to all of the Navajos.

In an apparent effort to reduce opposition between Navajos and Whites regarding the control and management of livestock and land-use in Navajo country, the Secretary of the Interior approved in 1952 a proposal of the Tribal Council (CA–30–52) to set up grazing committees which were to be composed of Navajos elected to office by Navajos. Their duties and responsibilities, however, did not include the right to determine the number of sheep-units individuals could maintain within a district; thus the grazing committees were deprived of any real authority. Ultimate control over land-use and livestock quotas was retained by the Government, since any changes in these matters had to have Tribal Council approval, and the Secretary of the Interior either approved or disapproved any Council resolution. Thus, even though Navajos have the right to choose which men (or women) will interpret and enforce grazing regulations in their area, the basic issue has remained unchanged and opposition still exists. The basic issue is that Navajos object to any outside agency having the authority to impose limitations on raising and grazing livestock, and this issue has become general in that it is used as a rallying point in all political statements and as a prime example of the Government's clumsiness in its attempt to change the life of the Navajo. In effect, the stock reduction program of the Government has become a symbol of Government interference with a Navajo way of life and, as such, can not be resolved within the existing political framework. Even though the Navajos and Whites are linked via a single structure or system of structures there is an imperfectly developed set of common understandings as to how this structure is to function.

The formation of chapters among the Navajo is clearly in contrast to either the Tribal Council or the grazing committees. Hunter's idea was to allow the Navajo to utilize preexisting patterns of political selection and social control in the operation of chapters. The form and the idea for chapters was supplied by Anglo-Americans, but the content of the sets of social relations was left up to the Navajo. There were other factors that contributed to the success of the chapter program.

There are strong indications that the Navajos in the Leupp jurisdiction felt a need to have a better means of contacting the Indian Service personnel during the late 1920's and early 1930's, for the surveys conducted during this period point out that the land was 100 percent overgrazed and had suffered greatly in terms of productivity because of droughts, thus making it very difficult for Navajos to grow a normal crop. The large number of Navajos who turned out for the general meetings held in Leupp by John Hunter are indicative of the need they felt about creating better lines of communication, and indicate at least their willingness to cooperate with the Government agents. Further evidence for the need Navajos felt about greater contact with Indian Agents is suggested by the fact that within a period of 3 to 4 years chapters were organized and operating in nearly 50 locations after they had been introduced to the Navajo in 1927. If the inference concerning the need felt by Navajos at this time is correct, then John Hunter's act of establishing a sociopolitical structure among Navajos to help him satisfy his needs as an administrator is truly an outstanding event in the history of the Government's efforts to direct programs of culture change among American Indians. Its importance lies in the fact that the chapter provided a structure linking Whites and Navajos, and it provided a basis for the development of a set of common understandings under conditions determined by the subordinate cultural group. Under Hunter's guidance the "town meeting" structural model was culturally integrated into the Navajo's existing sociopolitical system, and the Navajos were allowed to accept or reject the idea of a chapter. When they found it acceptable, they were allowed a wide choice in determining the meaning and function of the new structure.

At first, headmen of local groups of Navajos were contacted by Indian Agents to see if they were interested in forming a chapter; if the headmen showed an interest they were permitted to select the time, place, and leaders of the new organization. Hunter's instruction to his fieldmen were to "Let it roll" once a chapter got started, by which he meant that the Navajos were to decide who were to be their leaders; the Navajos were to be allowed to use their traditional way of selecting these leaders; the decisions made by a chapter were to be enforced only by Navajos within their traditional patterns of maintaining social and political control; and the Indian Agents (and their interpreters) were present at chapter meetings in the roll of guests rather than as political supervisors.

Many chapters began community projects such as building check dams or constructing a meeting hall in which to hold chapter meetings. These self-help community projects not only introduced Navajos to a host of new ideas, tools, and techniques, but were highly visible and tangible evidence to Navajos of cooperation on the community level of organization. In addition, these projects provided an additional setting in which Navajos were allowed to exercise their new set of relationships with Whites, for the Indian Service personnel were strongly advised to stay in the background and offer advice and assistance only when asked. The bosses of these community projects were the headmen of the local land-use community. Under these conditions of contact, each chapter was allowed to integrate new cultural elements at its own speed and under its own terms; the idea for a chapter was not forced upon any local group nor was the content of the contact situation determined by the agents of the Government.

The strength of the chapter program is attested to by the fact that during the 1930's and 1940's, when opposition to the Government's program of direct and forceful culture change regarding livestock reached a peak, chapters in many areas continued to function and hold meetings. Records are not available to determine the number of chapters that failed to continue, but by 1950 about 40 units were still operating. These 40 chapters represent about one-half of the number in operation during 1933 to 1934; that period of time during which the Government officially disassociated itself from the chapter program. Therefore, chapters continued without Government support during a period of considerable conflict between Navajos and Whites, and it is inferred that these new political structures had been sufficiently integrated into the Navajo culture—at least to the degree that beliefs, attitudes, and behavior patterns had been mutually adjusted among Whites and Navajos—to form a single system. The evidence for this inference is manifest in the statement by Henry Smith (see pp. 28 ff.) who said that chapter organizations were used throughout the voluntary stock reduction program by Soil Conservation Service personnel, Bureau of Indian Affairs employees, and by the Navajo Tribal Council members to explain and implement the program, even though the official policy of the Government was to ignore the chapters (see p. 38).

Officially, the Government recognized chapters again in 1955 when the Secretary of the Interior Department approved the council resolution (CJ–20–55) to include this "grassroots" political organization as a part of Navajo tribal government. The resolution placed chapters under a newly created Community Development Department of the Navajo Tribe. Under the direction of this tribal department a total of 96 chapters are currently operating in all parts of Navajo country, and over half of these units have new modern buildings in which to hold their meetings.

The function of the chapters today generally differs very little from that during the 1930's in that they still provide a place for discussion and dissemination of information. Also, in the places where new chapter houses are located they provide members the opportunity to see, use, and develop associations with many new cultural elements. The new buildings frequently have running water, butane heating units, flush toilets, washing machines, public address equipment, movie projectors, popcorn machines, soda pop dispensers, electric stoves, folding metal chairs, tile floors, sewing machines, welding equipment, flagpoles, and concrete walkways. They also provide opportunities for Navajos to meet, to talk with, to listen to, and to observe strangers who come to the meetings as tribal officials, Bureau of Indian Affairs officers, missionaries, anthropologists, newspapermen, tourists, politicians seeking votes for offices on the local school boards, or county, State and National political units.

The modern chapters also allow Navajos to gain additional experience in handling political principles and concepts such as majority rule, quorum, petition, and secret balloting under conditions they themselves determine and decide upon, rather than having the cultural content determined by members of the superordinate society (which is the case for the Navajo Tribal Council and the grazing committees).

In summary, the chapter organization provides a setting within which the process of incorporation of new cultural elements continues even though the Navajo are subject to a directed program of culture change. An aspect of this process of cultural integration is the incorporation of political principles and concepts derived from the Anglo-American culture; the major functions of the chapters within the Navajo political system is that they provide a structure that allows the transfer of Anglo-American principles of government to the Navajo culture with a minimum amount of opposition and conflict. The primary reason for the ease of transfer is that the Navajos have great freedom in applying their traditional meaning and function to the various social and political positions within the borrowed structure.

References

ALBERT, ETHEL M.
1956. The classification of values: a method and illustration. Amer. Anthropol., vol. 58, no. 2, pp. 221–248.

BENAVIDES, FRAY ALONZO DE
1945. Revised memorial of 1634, edited by F. Hodge, G. P. Hammond, and A. Rey. Albuquerque, N. Mex.

BENNETT, CAPT. F. T.
1870. Document. *In* "Report of the Commissioner of Indian Affairs" for the year 1869.

BRUGGE, DAVID M.
1963. Documentary references to a Navajo Naach'id in 1850. Ethnohistory, vol. 10, no. 2, pp. 186–188.

BUNKER, ROBERT
1956. Other men's skies. Bloomington, Ind.

CARR, MALCOLM; SPENCER, KATHERINE; and WOOLEY, DORIANE
1939. Navajo clans and marriage at Pueblo Alto. Amer. Anthropol., vol. 41, pp. 245–257.

COLLIER, MALCOLM CARR
1951. Local organization among the Navahos. Ph. D. thesis, Univ. Chicago [Unpublished.]

COMMISSIONER OF INDIAN AFFAIRS
1906. Annual Report of the Commissioner of Indian Affairs. Washington.

COUNCIL RESOLUTIONS OF THE NAVAJO TRIBE
1923–63. Navajo Tribe records office. Window Rock, Ariz.

DOZIER, EDWARD P.
1951. Resistance to acculturation and assimilation in an Indian Pueblo. Amer. Anthropol., vol. 53, no. 1, pp. 56–65.
1954. The Hopi-Tewa of Arizona. Univ. Calif. Publ. Amer. Archaeol. and Ethnol., vol. 44, no. 3, pp. 259–376.

EGGAN, FRED
1950. Social organization of the western Pueblos. Chicago.

FORRESTAL, PETER P.
1954. Benavides memorial of 1630. Academy Amer. Franciscan Hist. Washington.

FRANCISCAN FATHERS
1910. An ethnologic dictionary of the Navaho language. [Reprinted in 1929.] St. Michaels, Ariz.

GILMORE, FRANCES, and WETHERILL, LOUISA WADE
1953. Traders to the Navajos. Albuquerque, N. Mex.

GREEN, EILEEN
1957. Navajo chapter organization. Window Rock, Ariz. [Unpublished.]

HILL, WILLARD W.
1939. The agricultural and hunting methods of the Navaho Indians. Yale Univ. Publ. Anthropol., no. 18. New Haven, Conn.

HILL, WILLARD W.—Continued

1940a. Some Navaho culture changes during two centuries. Smithsonian Misc. Coll., vol. 100, pp. 395–416.

1940b. Some aspects of Navajo political structure. Plateau, vol. 13, no. 2, pp. 23–28.

HODGE, FREDERICK WEBB

1895. The early Navajo and Apache. Amer. Anthropol., o.s., vol. 8, pp. 223–240.

HUGHES, JOHN T.

1961. Doniphan's expedition, 1847. *In* Perspectives in American Indian culture change, edited by Edward H. Spicer. Chicago.

KELEHER, WILLIAM A.

1952. Turmoil in New Mexico, 1846–1868. Santa Fe, N. Mex.

KELLY, HENRY W.

1941. Franciscan missions of New Mexico, 1740–1760. New Mex. Hist. Rev., vol. 16, pp. 41–70.

KEUR, DOROTHY LOUISE

1941. Big Bead Mesa, an archaeological study of Navajo acculturation 1745–1812. Soc. Amer. Archaeol., Mem. no. 1.

KIMBALL, SOLON T.

1950. Future problems in Navajo administration. Human Organization, vol. 9, no. 2, pp. 21–24.

KIMBALL, SOLON T., and PROVINSE, JOHN H.

1942. Navajo social organization in land use and planning. Applied Anthropol., vol. 1, no. 4, pp. 18–25.

KLUCKHOHN, CLYDE

1944. Navajo witchcraft. Boston.

KLUCKHOHN, CLYDE, and LEIGHTON, DOROTHEA

1946. The Navaho. [Reprinted in 1951.] Cambridge, Mass.

LEFT-HANDED MEXICAN CLANSMAN, *see* YOUNG and MORGAN, 1952.

LETHERMAN (LETTERMAN), JONATHAN

1856. Sketch of the Navajo Tribe of Indians, Territory of New Mexico. 10th Ann. Rep. Smithsonian Institution for the year 1855.

LEVY, JERROLD E.

1962. Community organization of the western Navajo. Amer. Anthropol., vol. 64, pp. 781–801.

MATTHEWS, WASHINGTON

1890. The gentile system of the Navajo Indians. Jour. Amer. Folklore, vol. 3, pp. 89–110.

MCKINLEY COUNTY REPUBLICAN

1905. Issue of December 16. Gallup, N. Mex.

NAVAJO RESERVATION CENTRAL GRAZING COMMITTEE

1953. Duties and responsibilities. Window Rock, Ariz.

1957. Duties and responsibilities. Window Rock.

1961. Central grazing committee record. Window Rock.

1962. Duties and responsibilities. Window Rock.

NAVAJO TRIBAL CODE

1962. Navajo Tribal Code, vols. 1 and 2. Orford, N.H.

RAPOPORT, ROBERT N.

1954. Changing Navajo religious values. Peabody Mus. Amer. Archaeol. and Ethnol., Pap., vol. 41, no. 2. Cambridge, Mass.

REEVE, FRANK D.

1937. The federal Indian policy in New Mexico, 1858–1880. N. Mex. Hist. Rev., vol. 12, no. 3, pp. 218–269.

1938. The federal Indian policy in New Mexico 1858–1880. N. Mex. Hist. Rev., vol. 13, no. 1, pp. 14–49.

1939. The government and the Navaho, 1848–1858. N. Mex. Hist. Rev., vol. 14, no. 1, pp. 82–114.

1941. The government and the Navaho 1878–1883. N. Mex. Hist. Rev., vol. 16, no. 3, pp. 275–312.

1943. The government and the Navaho 1883–1888. N. Mex. Hist. Rev., vol. 18, no. 1, pp. 17–51.

1946. A Navaho struggle for land. N. Mex. Hist. Rev., vol. 21, no. 1, pp. 1–21.

1957. Seventeenth-century Navaho-Spanish relations. N. Mex. Hist. Rev., vol. 32, pp. 36–52.

1959. The Navaho-Spanish peace: 1720's–1770's. N. Mex. Hist. Rev., vol. 34, no. 1, pp. 9–40.

1960. Navaho-Spanish diplomacy, 1770–1790. N. Mex. Hist. Rev., vol. 35, no. 3, pp. 200–233.
REICHARD, GLADYS A.
1928. Social life of the Navaho Indians. Columbia Univ. Contr. Anthropol., no. 7. New York.
ROSS, WILLIAM T.
1955. Navajo kinship and social organization; with special reference to a transitional community. Ph. D. thesis, Univ. Chicago.
SASAKI, TOM T.
1960. Fruitland, New Mexico: a Navaho community in transition. Ithaca, N.Y.
SAVELLE, MAX
1942. The foundations of American civilization. New York.
SHEPARDSON, MARY
1960. Developing political process among the Navajo Indians. Ph. D. thesis, Univ. California at Berkeley.
1963. Navajo ways in government. Amer. Anthropol. Assoc., Mem. no. 96, vol. 65, no. 3, pt. 2.
SPICER, EDWARD H.,
1952. Sheepmen and technicians. *In* "Human problems in technological change," edited by Edward H. Spicer. New York.
1954. Spanish-Indian acculturation in the southwest. Part 1. Amer. Anthropol., vol. 56, no. 4, pp. 663–684.
SPICER, EDWARD H., editor
1952. Human problems in technological change. New York.
1961. Perspectives in American Indian culture change. Chicago.
STEPHEN, ALEXANDER M.
1893. The Navajo. Amer. Anthropol., o.s., vol. 6, no. 4, pp. 345–362.
THOMAS, ALFRED B.
1940. The Plains Indians of New Mexico, 1751–1778. Albuquerque.
UNDERHILL, RUTH
1953. Here come the Navaho! Bur. Indian Aff., Branch of Educ. Indian Life and Customs Publ. 8. Washington.
1956. The Navajos. Norman, Okla.
UNITED STATES GOVERNMENT
1946. Treaty between the United States of America and the Navajo Tribe of Indians 1868. Phoenix, Ariz.
VAN VALKENBURGH, RICHARD
1936. Navajo common law I. Museum Notes, vol. 9, no. 4. Mus. Northern Ariz., Flagstaff.
1938. A short history of the Navajo people. [Mimeographed.] Window Rock.
1945. The government of the Navajos. Arizona Quart., vol. 1, no. 4, pp. 63–73.
1946. Last powwow of the Navajo. The Desert Mag., vol. 10, no. 1, pp. 4–7.
1948. Navaho Naat'aani. The Kiva, vol. 13, no. 2, pp. 14–23.
1954. Navajo common law, I, II, III. *In* "Navajo Customs." Mus. Northern Ariz., Reprint Ser. no. 6. Flagstaff.
VOGT, EVON Z.
1951. Navaho veterans. Peabody Mus. Amer. Archaol. and Ethnol., Pap. vol. 41, no. 1. Cambridge, Mass.
1961. The Navaho. *In* Perspectives in American Indian culture change, edited by Edward H. Spicer. Chicago.
VOGT, EVON Z.; KLUCKHOHN, CLYDE; and MCCOMBE, LEONARD
1951. Navaho means people. Cambridge, Mass.
WEBER, FATHER ANSELM
1914. The Navajo Indians: a statement of facts. St. Michaels Mission, Ariz.
WEBER, ANSELM; HARTUNG, FREDERICK; and FISCHER, EGBERT; et al. O.F.M.
1908. Die Franziskaner Mission unter den Navajo-Indianern. Der Sendbote des Göttlichen Herzens Jesu, no. 35, pp. 36–37.
WILKEN, ROBERT L.
1955. Anselm Weber, O.F.M. Milwaukee, Wisc.
WILSON, GODFREY, AND WILSON, MONICA
1945. The analysis of social change. Cambridge, England.
WYMAN, LELAND C., and KLUCKHOHN, CLYDE
1938. Navaho classification of their song ceremonials. Amer. Anthropol. Assoc., Mem., no. 50.

YOUNG, ROBERT W.

1956. The Navajo yearbook of planning in action. Report No. 5, 1955–1956. Window Rock, Ariz.

1957. The Navajo yearbook of planning in action. Report No. 6, 1956–57. Window Rock.

1961. The Navajo yearbook of planning in action. Report No. 8, 1959–61. Window Rock.

YOUNG, ROBERT W., and MORGAN, WILLIAM, editors

1949. The Ramah Navahos by the son of Former Many Beads. Dept. Interior, Navajo Hist. Ser. No. 1. Washington.

1951. A vocabulary of colloquial Navaho. Dept. Interior, Washington.

1952. The trouble at Round Rock. Dept. Interior, Navajo Hist. Ser. No. 2. Washington.

Appendix

RESOLUTION OF THE ADVISORY COMMITTEE OF THE NAVAJO TRIBAL COUNCIL

ACO-149-59 (COPY)

APPROVING ELECTION PROCEDURES OF CHAPTER OFFICERS

WHEREAS:

1. There is now no standard approved election procedures for the election of Chapter Officers and consequently there is much confusion in the elections of such officers at this time, and

2. The Chapter Presidents at their annual chapter meeting held on September 2–4 and 17 and 18, 1959, have thoroughly discussed and approved the attached procedures for election of Chapter Officers, and recommended the approval and implementation of these procedures by the Advisory Committee, and

3. The Advisory Committee feels that the election procedures for Chapter Officers are desirable and necessary for proper administration of the Navajo Chapter organizations.

NOW THEREFORE BE IT RESOLVED THAT:

1. The attached procedures for election of Chapter Officers be and they are hereby approved as standard election procedures for Chapter Officers of the Navajo Tribal Council.

CERTIFICATION

I hereby certify that the foregoing resolution was duly considered by the Advisory Committee of the Navajo Tribal Council at a duly called meeting at Window Rock, Arizona, at which a quorum was present and that same was passed by a vote of 9 in favor and 0 opposed, this 2nd day of October, 1959.

/s/ Paul Jones
Chairman
Navajo Tribal Council

321-627—70——6

PROCEDURES FOR ELECTION OF CHAPTER OFFICERS

1. NAME: This chapter is known as the______________________________
   CHAPTER,____
   (place)

2. OFFICERS: The chapter shall have an elected president, vice-president, and secretary.

3. DUTIES OF OFFICERS:

   a. *President.* The president shall preside at all meetings, have power to call meetings with consent of the other officers, attend tribal meetings and represent the chapter as called upon to do so. He shall have a vote in all chapter elections.

   b. *Vice-President.* The vice-president shall perform the duties of the president in case of disability or absence of the president, and shall have a vote in chapter elections.

   c. *Secretary.* The secretary shall prepare written minutes or reports of all meetings, carry on correspondence, and act as treasurer of chapter funds. He shall have a vote in chapter elections.

4. TERMS OF OFFICE: The term of office for each officer shall be 4 years and the regular election of chapter officers shall be held in July of each tribal election year.

5. ELECTION: Election of officers shall be carried out in the following manner:

   a. At least 15 days before the date established for the election, public notice shall be posted announcing the date, place, and time of the election, and the chapter shall be so advised by the president in the regular meeting next preceding the election.

   b. The election shall be carried out in a duly called meeting of the chapter at which at least 25 adult members over 21 years of age of the chapter shall be present.

   c. Nominations for each office shall be made from the floor, and the president shall allow any number of nominations for each office. Election for the office of president shall be completed before nominations are opened for vice-president, and similarly shall be completed before nominations are opened for secretary.

   d. Election shall be by standing vote for each nominee.

   e. Each adult member of the chapter shall be allowed one vote when present at the election.

   f. A plurality vote shall elect each officer. In the event of a tie vote, a brief recess shall be declared, after which another vote shall be taken on the tying candidates only. In the event of a second tie vote, the incumbent shall continue in office until the next following meeting, at which another vote shall be taken on the tying candidates.

6. ASSUMPTION OF OFFICE: Newly-elected officers shall take office at the meeting next following their election.

7. VACATING OF OFFICE: In the event of death, disability, resignation, removal of an officer from the community, or ineligibility of an officer his office shall be declared vacant by the presiding officer at the next regular meeting, and an election to fill the vacancy shall be announced and carried out in the manner prescribed in section 5 above.

8. RECALL: Any officer of this chapter may be removed from office by the following procedure:
   a. Upon the presentation to him of a written petition signed by at least twenty adult members of the chapter the presiding officer of the chapter shall read aloud (or cause to be read) such petition at the next regular meeting of the chapter, which shall be called within 30 days of receipt of the petition by the presiding officer, and the presiding officer shall announce an election to fill the office of the officer so recalled by the petition, provided however, that the incumbent shall stand for re-election *if he so desires.*
   b. At the next duly called meeting of the chapter, which shall occur within 30 days after the reading of the petition of recall, an election shall be held to fill the position of the officer so recalled and such election shall be carried out in accordance with provisions of sections 5 and 6, and his term of office shall continue until the next regular election.

9. CERTIFICATION OF ELECTION: Within ten days after an election by the Chapter, the secretary shall prepare and transmit a report of said election to the Tribal Officers at Window Rock.

10. ELIGIBILITY: No elected delegate serving in the Navajo Tribal Council shall be eligible to serve as a Chapter officer.

11. APPEAL OF ELECTION: A disputed election of any officer of this chapter may be appealed to the chapter organization by the aggrieved party, and the decision of the chapter shall be final and binding. A report of the decision shall be submitted to the Advisory Committee within 10 days after said decision.

12. ENABLING CLAUSE: *repeal, amendment* The foregoing bylaws of the ______________ chapter shall be in full force and effect from the date of their adoption by the Advisory Committee. Upon a vote of ⅔ majority of the members of a Chapter at a duly called meeting, to repeal or amend any section of these bylaws, the change will become effective as to this chapter upon approval of the Advisory Committee.

____
Chapter President

____
Chapter Vice-President

____
Chapter Secretary

____
Councilman

____
Grazing Committee Member

8. Recall. Any officer of this chapter may be removed from office for the following reasons: [illegible]

[illegible]

[illegible]

9. [illegible]

[illegible]

[illegible]

[illegible]

[illegible]

Councilman

Ranking Committee Member

Plates 1–10

321–627—70——7

PLATE 1

Early chapter activities. *Top left,* John G. Hunter. *Top right,* Travel conditions on the Navajo Reservation during the 1930's. *Center,* Chapter members and guests lined up for a meal at the 1930 dedication ceremony of the Kin Li Chee Chapter House. *Bottom,* Last-minute addition of chairs to accommodate the crowd at a 1931 chapter meeting.

321-627-70——8

PLATE 2

The Kin Li Chee Chapter. *Top,* An early (1929) chapter meeting held at Kin Li Chee. (Courtesy J. L. Rush). *Center,* the Kin Li Chee Chapter House in 1931. *Bottom,* A tug-of-war game during the 1931 dedication of the Kin Li Chee Chapter House.

PLATE 3

The Fort Defiance Chapter. *Top*, Navajo hogans near Fort Defiance in 1930. *Center*, The construction of the Fort Defiance Chapter House in 1933. (Courtesy J. L. Rush.) *Bottom*, Interior of the Fort Defiance Chapter House; a display of crafts in 1934. (Courtesy J. L. Rush.)

PLATE 4

The Rock Point Chapter; construction of a diversion dam. *Top*, The president of the Rock Point Chapter standing in the direct foreground during the evening meal for the workers. (Courtesy J. L. Rush.) *Center*, Rock Point Chapter members who donated their labor to the building of the diversion dam. *Bottom*, Preparation by chapter members for the cement setting forms. (Courtesy J. L. Rush.)

PLATE 5

The Rock Point Chapter; construction of a diversion dam. *Top*, The left side of the diversion dam with the cement form and steel reinforcements in place. *Bottom*, The Rock Point diversion dam after completion, showing the spillway. (Courtesy J. L. Rush.)

PLATE 6

The Teastoh and Mexican Springs Chapters. *Top,* The president of the Teastoh Chapter addressing chapter members at a meeting in 1959. *Bottom,* A member of the Mexican Springs Chapter assisting in building the modern chapter house in 1961.

PLATE 7

The Shonto and Lukachukai Chapters. *Top*, Local labor at the Shonto Chapter moving a painting platform in 1958. (Courtesy Navajo Tribe.) *Bottom*, The isolated setting of the Lukachukai Chapter House, completed in 1958, is typical of many modern chapter house locations. (Courtesy Navajo Tribe.)

PLATE 8

The dedication of a chapter house. *Top*, Final instructions on the day prior to the dedication, in 1958, of the Steamboat Chapter House (Courtesy Navajo Tribe.) *Bottom*, The performance of the Blessing Way Ceremony, for a new chapter house, by two medicine men and an assistant. (Courtesy Navajo Tribe.)

PLATE 9

The dedication of a chapter house. *Top*, The ceremonial raising of the American flag during the dedication of a chapter house. *Bottom*, A guest speaker, Scott Preston, vice-chairman of the Navajo Tribal Council, addresses a 1959 meeting of the Mariana Lake Chapter.

PLATE 10

The St. Michaels and Ganado Chapters. *Top*, The 1933 dedication of the St. Michaels Chapter House. (Courtesy J. L. Rush.) *Bottom*, The Ganado Chapter House, completed in 1933 and still in use for chapter meetings. (Courtesy J. L. Rush.)

Index